GOOD HOUSEKEEPING
Everyday
ETIQUETTE

GOOD HOUSEKEEPING
Everyday
ETIQUETTE

A comprehensive guide to:

Common courtesies

How to be a perfect guest

Entertaining

PLUS

How to cope with formal
occasions

ELIZABETH MARTYN

EBURY PRESS LONDON

Published by Ebury Press
an imprint of Century Hutchinson Ltd
Brookmount House 62–65 Chandos Place, Covent Garden, London
WC2N 4NW

First impression 1989

British Library Cataloguing in Publication Data
Martyn, Elizabeth
   Good housekeeping everyday etiquette: a comprehensive guide to
   common courtesies, how to be a perfect guest, entertaining... –
   (GH practical library).
   1. Etiquette – Manuals
   I. Title
   395

ISBN 0-85223-723-5

Consultants:
Cassandra Kent, Consumer Affairs Editor,
Good Housekeeping

Betty Kenward, Social Editor,
Harper's & Queen

Edited by Sarah Bailey
and Heather Rocklin
Designed by Gwyn Lewis

Filmset from author's disk by Textype Typesetters, Cambridge
Printed and bound in Great Britain at The Bath Press, Avon

Contents

Acknowledgements

The publishers wish to thank Cassandra Kent and Betty Kenward for their invaluable help and advice.

Civility costs nothing and buys everything.

Lady Mary Wortley Montagu,
Letter to the Countess of Bute, 30 May 1756

Introduction

Etiquette will never go out of fashion as long as people get married and buried, meet each other, visit friends, throw parties, go to work, eat out.

Knowing how to behave in any situation makes you feel more confident and puts the people around you at ease. And that's why etiquette exists: to oil the wheels of social exchange and make life pleasanter and more relaxed for everyone.

This book won't tell you how to make out a place card for the wife of a younger son of a baronet, or whether a Rear-Admiral takes precedence over a High Sheriff. But if you've ever dithered over whether to shake hands or kiss; wondered how to ease lingering guests politely towards the door; struggled to compose a letter of complaint; felt tongue-tied at a party or hung up when a machine answered the phone, you'll find plenty of help here.

Times change and etiquette changes with them. Medieval books explained how to behave when sharing a bed with strangers in an inn, or defecating in the street (very rude to talk to someone engaged in this activity); while the Victorians and Edwardians were hidebound by a mass of do's and don'ts designed to foster class differences and which they ignored at their peril.

Today the move away from rigid rules makes it much easier to gauge the right way to behave because there are fewer out and out 'wrongs'. Of course there are still a few situations where inflexible rules apply, although these are mainly concerned with official functions. But nine times out of ten, the way you choose to behave is up to you, with one very important proviso: that you keep firmly in mind the basis on which etiquette has grown up, which is the need always to consider other people's feelings first. Remember that, and you can use most of the other advice in this book as a pointer towards possible ways of dealing with different situations. Which option you choose, or whether you adopt another style which is completely your own, matters very little, because social behaviour is far freer now than ever before. After all, it has to be, to accommodate the vast range of cultures and lifestyles that exist side by side in society.

Some people, for instance, are very informal and outgoing by nature, while others prefer to be a bit more reserved and formal. Younger people stand on ceremony less often than their parents. Habits vary too in different parts of the country. Behaviour which is commonplace in the capital – the social kiss; arriving later than the stated time – is unconventional elsewhere. Just remember the groundrule of consideration for others, and when in doubt take your lead from those around you and err on the side of caution.

Etiquette is a skill that's easily learned, and it reaps the reward of other people's appreciation whenever you put it into practice. After all, good manners enhance the quality of life. It's a pleasure to spend time with people who are reliably courteous and considerate; and pleasant too, to feel that you will always know what to do or say in any circumstances, mundane or extraordinary.

1

Everyday courtesies

Etiquette in the broad sense of courteous, thoughtful behaviour, isn't something to be wheeled out on special occasions and put aside the rest of the time. A little consideration
for others goes a long way towards improving the quality of
life and lowering stress in numerous situations, every day of
the week. Families co-exist more calmly with a polite
approach on all sides, and courtesy helps smooth the path
too in 101 common-or-garden transactions that take place in
shops or restaurants, on public transport, in the office, on the
telephone.

Public proprieties

Smoking   Fast becoming less and less acceptable, so always
look around for signs before you light up. Some cinemas and
restaurants permit smoking in designated areas only and a
growing number outlaw it completely. It's no longer considered unladylike to smoke in the street, but it doesn't look
particularly attractive, and is certainly inconsiderate to non-
smokers walking behind who find themselves unwillingly
swathed in fumes. Smoking is particularly unpleasant for
others in a crowd of people, where it's impossible to man-
eouvre away from the smoke, and there is also a risk of being
accidentally burned.

Smokers should always ask if there is any objection to
smoking – and they shouldn't even ask while anyone else is
eating. A non-smoker may justifiably object to people smoking in his or her home or car, since the smell lingers on. If this
applies to you and you decide to put your foot down, be
braced for guilt-inducing cries of protest from deprived
smokers. If you are happy for friends to smoke, provide
frequently emptied ashtrays, keep the room ventilated and

burn a large candle in the room to help disperse the fumes.

Smokers should be aware of what is happening to the smoke and ash they create. Hold lit cigarettes away from others, blow smoke away from their faces and make sure that none is drifting away to annoy people at an adjacent table or seat.

Sneezing and coughing It's not always easy for women to find a home for a handkerchief. Tuck one up the sleeve of your jumper if it ruins the immaculate line of your jacket or trousers, or carry a discreet wad of tissues – neater and easier to stash away in handbag or pocket and readily disposable after use.

It ought to go without saying that you should cover your mouth with handkerchief, or at the very least your hand, when you cough or sneeze, and turn your head away from other people. Unfortunately, some people seem to enjoy sharing their violent expulsions with those round about.

Swearing Swear words are common currency these days, and expressions that our mothers wouldn't have understood issue regularly from the mouths of schoolchildren or TV stars. Be that as it may, many people still find swearing offensive and even if you eff-and-blind merrily in the privacy of your own four walls you should censor your language when talking to others.

Make-up Women can re-apply lipstick or lightly powder their noses in public with impunity, and it's sometimes easier to do this quickly at the table in a restaurant, say, than make a special trip to the Ladies. However, there is something distinctly unappealing about watching a woman apply a full make-up in public, with all the attendant facial contortions. Anything other than basic running repairs are better tackled in private.

Arguing We've all watched or listened horrified as a major row explodes in public. It's as embarrassing and unpleasant for onlookers as it is for the combatants, even if they are too far gone to care at the time. Saving a row until you get home is not just courteous to others, it gives you both a chance to cool down, and decide if whatever sparked off the disagreement is really worth arguing about.

Q *In a wine bar the other day a man at the next table lit cigarette after cigarette, oblivious to the fact that his smoke was billowing straight across our table. We tried coughing loudly and fanning ourselves vigorously, but he didn't take the hint since he was far too engrossed in his conversation. What should we have done?*

A Interrupted him politely and pointed out that the smoke was bothering you. The direct approach is usually far more effective because it demands a response, unlike broad 'hints' which are too easy to ignore. However, if he didn't react to your request, you might then have been obliged to move to another table, or even complain to the management.

Manners between men and women

Should men still walk on the outside of the pavement to protect their female companions from the mud splashed up by passing carriages? This is one old custom that has died hard, and is still common practice. Many men also automatically stand back and give a woman precedence through a door, although a well-mannered woman should open a door for a man if it happens to be easier for her to do so, or carry her own bag if he is already laden.

These things depend very much on the attitudes and background of the individuals, but whatever a woman thinks about such minor courtesies she should accept them gracefully if they are offered, or at the very least refuse them politely. 'That's very kind, but I can manage thank you', goes down better than a surly 'I can manage perfectly well by myself'.

Commuters have developed rules of their own to cope with the packed conditions in which they travel. If there is a rush for one seat, many men will let a woman win. However, possession is nine-tenths of the law, and a man who is already seated is unlikely to offer his seat to a woman who is standing. An exception might be made if she is is obviously pregnant, but even then it's just as likely to be another woman who gives up her seat. People of either sex who are infirm, aged or weighed down with young children always deserve to be offered a seat by whoever's nearest.

Q *Should a man let a woman go first down a flight of stairs, on a bus, for instance?*

A Strictly speaking he should go first in order to catch her (or provide a soft landing!) if she should fall, and for the same reason he should let her precede him when they are going *up* a flight of stairs. But this custom is not always observed these days.

Polite talk

Gossip Words are powerful implements and can all too easily wound or distress. Malicious gossip is unforgiveable. Don't listen to it, or spread it. Innocent gossip may be entertaining, but is just as potentially damaging. It's no fun to be the object of others' speculations and discover that some spurious story is being passed round about you. Be careful what you say about others and to whom you say it. It is very easy to put two and two together and make five, so beware of making assumptions. There is often an innocent explanation for unusual behaviour and even if there isn't it benefits no one to spread rumour and innuendo.

Discretion A friend who can really be trusted to keep a secret is rare and valuable. If you are told – or discover – a fact about someone else which you know or suspect they want kept private, you should respect that, no matter how tempting it is to spread your story far and wide. This applies all the more to facts acquired in the course of work, and if you have access to medical, financial or other personal details of people, these should be kept totally confidential (*see also* OFFICE ETIQUETTE, page 23).

Jokes and leg-pulling Be aware of other people's sensibilities, and make sure that they share your sense of humour or can take a joke before you start trying to raise a laugh at their expense. Exercise special care with jokes about race, religion and sexuality. Even if not directed at a particular individual they may be found offensive by listeners.

The world is divided into those who think practical jokes hilarious and those whose flesh creeps with appalled embarrassment at the thought. Kissagrams, whoopee cushions, exploding tins of peanuts and the like should only be inflicted on those who will appreciate them (once they've got over the shock) and not laid on for the delight of onlookers if the recipient is likely to be dismayed rather than amused.

Moods Everyone has bad moods from time to time, but it is not only possible but highly desirable to keep these to yourself until they pass. There's no reason to impose your ill temper, depression or sorrow on others and people who snap, kick the furniture, shout or weep at no provocation quickly exhaust the patience of friends or colleagues.

Compliments A compliment pleasantly and gratefully accepted can give almost as big a boost to the giver as the receiver. On the other hand, a compliment greeted with a grunt, or a denial – 'What, this old thing?' – makes both parties feel uncomfortable, and the giver wish that he or she hadn't bothered. A genuine smile and a 'Thank you' are all that's needed to accept a compliment. There's no need to add any more unless you want to, nor to pay the other person a compliment in return, which can devalue the original remark.

Little white lies Useful as delaying tactics. 'Can I ring you back – I can't find my diary?', gives you time to think whether you want to go or not, and if so, on what terms. 'Thank you for a lovely evening/weekend/party' can be followed by something vague which leaves room for free interpretation: 'We did enjoy meeting your friends *[apart from that awful drunken man]*', 'The food was delicious *[or might have been if you'd cooked it properly]*'. Small economies with the truth along these lines hurt no one as long as the recipient is kept unaware of your true feelings, so be careful who you share these with. Bigger lies are dangerous. Avoid them.

Q *My 14-year-old son's best friend keeps borrowing small sums of money, but although he promises to return the cash, he never does. What's the best way for my son to deal with this? He and the other boy are otherwise very good friends, and it would be a shame if they fell out.*

A Your son just needs to say: 'John, could I have back that money I loaned you please.' If he finds it easier, he could give some reason for needing the money immediately, such as having a present to buy.

Q *I made a horrible gaffe the other day at a party, when I said something uncomplimentary about my daughter's class teacher, only to be told later that his girlfriend was in the room and had overheard me. Should I have apologized to her?*

A Since the damage had already been done, an attempt to explain or apologize might well have made matters worse. The only thing you might have done to ease matters would have been to say something complimentary about the teacher later on.

Q *A colleague often tells me how he boosts his office expenses claim by including receipts for meals bought for friends, or itemizing 'taxis' which he hasn't taken. What should I do? I don't approve of what he's doing, but neither do I want to 'tell tales'.*

A Make your opinion known to your colleague, by telling him that you take a dim view of his cheating. Sooner or later he is likely to be caught out, and there's no need for you to interfere by telling the boss.

Q *My plump friend makes a habit of squeezing herself into clothes which are a size too small, and which serve only to emphasize her spare tyre. Last week she asked me if I liked her new dress. Should I have told the truth and said it would look better in a larger size?*

A If you were out shopping with your friend when she asked your opinion, or you were *sure* that the dress could have been changed, you could have said tactfully that it looked a little tight and suggested that the next size up might be more comfortable. But if you saw the dress on its first outing, when it would have been too late to change it, then it would be kinder not to spoil your friend's enjoyment by telling her that the dress didn't fit.

Employing help at home

Whether you employ a full-time live-in nanny or have help once a week with the housework, you'll need to establish a way of dealing with employees – even if they come to feel more like friends – that is as comfortable and easy as possible for you both.

Top of your list of priorities when searching for your right-hand person, is to find someone with whom you can communicate well and to whom you warm readily. References, experience and willingness are all very important of course, but if your employee gets your back up every time he or she enters the room, your relationship is always going to be under serious strain. So, whether you use advertisements, agencies or word of mouth to find a helper, always arrange a meeting before you commit yourself.

Before any hopefuls come for an interview, make up your mind exactly what duties are involved. How many hours work a week are you looking for and can you be flexible over which hours and/or days are worked? Do you expect a cleaner to do ironing and washing up, or a nanny to help out with light housework? Make all this plain at the interview and ensure that you reach an agreement on exactly what is required. If your helper is going to spend a lot of time unsupervized in your house, what are you going to do about keys, visiting friends, use of the phone, meals and drinks? All these points need to be sorted out early on.

Ask for references and follow them up. And take people on for a 'trial period', which once completed to the satisfaction of both sides, can lead to a more formal arrangement with a stated period of notice.

Don't fight shy of talking about money. Payment should be discussed at the initial interview, not just how much, but the details of how you intend to pay – weekly, daily, in cash or with a cheque. With 'proper' employees such as nannies or housekeepers, you will have to pay National Insurance and income tax. Consult your local Inland Revenue office about the best way of doing this.

Any problems that come up once your employee has started work should be tackled immediately. Point out tactfully why you are unhappy and suggest a way of solving the problem. Do this politely and reasonably, and give the person a reasonable opportunity to improve or change before you embark on any further action.

In the last resort you may have no option but to fire your employee. This is never pleasant, and is best done swiftly once you've made up your mind. Give your reasons in a way which brooks no argument. Don't enter into a discussion of the whys and wherefores if you can possibly avoid it, and don't apologize. In these situations it's often easier all round to offer pay in lieu of notice so that your ex-employee can leave immediately. You should tell him or her whether or not you will be prepared to give a reference in future.

Au pairs   Au pairs are usually employed through an agency, who should check references and sort out details of payments, pocket money and so on. Agencies will usually guarantee to replace a girl who is unsatisfactory or unhappy with your family.

If an au pair steals or runs up a huge bill you are entitled to send her home. The agency may arrange this for you. If you have acquired an au pair privately you can always ring her parents if problems arise. The threat of this may well act as a deterrent. And you can put a lock on your phone so that only specified numbers can be dialled.

Babysitters Give a realistic estimate of your return time and provide some refreshment if you are going to be out all evening. Leave a contact number for emergencies, and ring home at an agreed time to check up if you are anxious. Teenage babysitters should be promised a lift, taxi or escort home if you are going to be back late. In return your baby-sitter should know and respect your rules about having friends round while babysitting and using (or not using) the phone. Agree payment in advance and have the cash ready. You will probably have to pay more after midnight.

Q *I suspect that my cleaner, who is left in the house alone while we are out at work, has been searching through the documents and letters in my desk. What should I do?*

A As you don't know for sure that your cleaner has been nosy it would be difficult to confront him or her. Lock away any private papers in future and keep an eye open for evidence of outright dishonesty. It is always important to lock up private papers and jewellery, and also fairer on the people working for you.

Q *I had an interview recently for a twice-weekly babysitting job and was offered the job. But the house was so dirty and the children so ill-behaved that I said I would consider the offer and let the couple know. I never rang back because I didn't know what to say. What should I have done?*

A You didn't need to give any reason for turning the job down, but it would have been polite to have rung and said you had decided not take it, or that something else had come up. Then they would have known that they had to look elsewhere.

Children

Yours When children accompany you on a visit make sure they bring a toy or two with which to amuse themselves while the adults are talking. Don't let them clamber over the furniture or pick up delicate objects. If something gets broken, offer to replace it, and if your offer is refused buy a small gift as an apology instead. By all means include children in the conversation if they are old enough to be interested, but teach them not to interrupt other people.

Children should know how to greet people and what to say when introduced (*see* INTRODUCTIONS, page 50). When visitors come to your home, keep an eye open to make sure that they are happy talking to your children. Some people, especially those who don't have children of their own, find dealing with kids for any length of time quite a strain, and may need help or rescue.

All children occasionally make a scene or tantrum when away from home. Try to react calmly even if you are tempted to shout or even administer a slap. Use distraction techniques to avert a crisis whenever possible.

Other people's When visiting friends with children, don't take sweets to give to the kids, as many parents object to their offspring consuming too many sugary foods. A small toy or coloured pencils are good alternatives, or you could ask your friends what the children are allowed. Should a friend's child start clambering on the furniture in your home, or be in danger of breaking something, firmly tell him or her to stop and if that fails ask the parent to intervene.

Don't ignore children, even if you are not used to talking to them. Quite young children will happily chatter to you, and older ones can be surprisingly interesting to talk to. Remember too that even if a child is silently playing in the room where adults are talking, he or she is probably taking in a lot more of what is being said than you imagine.

Q *At a family party my eight-year-old niece jumped up and down on my favourite old sofa and took no notice of her mother's warnings that she would break it. When they'd gone I realised that the arm of the sofa had come loose, and it has cost me a fair amount of money to have it repaired. I haven't told my sister-in-law about this – should I have?*

A You most certainly should, and she should have refunded you for the repairs. In fact, your niece is old enough to understand the value of other people's property and might usefully have been asked by her mother to contribute to the cost. It might initially have been easier to have raised the point with your brother, rather than your sister-in-law.

Pets

Yours Dogs should be trained to keep their bark down when people when friends arrive, once reassured that the house is not being burgled. Don't allow any pet to jump up at a visitor unless you are sure that the visitor is happy to be covered in hair, well-licked or gently clawed. Not everyone will be pleased to see you arrive accompanied by your pet, so check first. If your pet makes a mess on someone else's floor, it's your job to apologize profusely – and clear it up.

Other people's Tell friends about any allergy you have before you visit so that they can arrange to keep pets out of the way. Speak up bravely if you are not keen on cats and dogs, and ask your hosts to keep their pets under control if you are being harassed. Don't feed titbits to other people's pets without the owner's permission. Guide dogs in particular should never be given extra 'snacks', as they are specially trained not to scavenge or accept titbits and are kept on a careful diet for health reasons.

Q *I like my friend's dog, but not his habit of forcefully thrusting his cold wet nose up my skirt whenever we meet. My friend appears to think that this is just a sign of affection on the part of Tubby (the dog). How can I get the message across?*

A Next time you meet, don't give Tubby a chance – grab him firmly, and push him away repeatedly, saying loudly 'NO', until he gives up. Tell your friend that fond as you are of Tubby, there are limits to the amount of canine affection you can tolerate.

The world of work

Applying for a job   Your letter of application represents that vital first chance to create a favourable impression on a potential employer. Make the letter short, straightforward and neatly typed (or handwritten if the advert requests this). Attach a clearly laid out and comprehensive CV. A fresh top copy of your CV is better than a tatty photostat which has obviously done the rounds, and worth the extra time it takes to prepare.

Use the letter to express interest in the job, and bring the reader's attention to any particularly relevant experience, referring him or her to your CV for more detail. Explain too why you are applying, but choose a reason connected with your positive feelings about the company or type of work, rather than the salary or closeness to home.

Re-read the advertisement carefully before you send off your application. Make sure you have enclosed everything requested, assured the company that you have the qualifications/experience asked for, and addressed the letter to the correct person (check the spelling).

The interview   Do your homework before an interview. Find out as much as you can about the company and the job for which you are applying. An interview has a dual purpose, in that it allows you to find out about your potential employers, as well as giving them a look at you. Leave plenty of time to get to the interview so that you have time for a few calming deep breaths before it begins. Don't be afraid to express your point of view, or to pause before answering a tricky question. Go prepared with a few questions of your own. Note them down in advance and refer to them during the interview if your memory tends to desert you at stressful moments.

References Former employers, fellow members of any local committees to which you belong, professional friends – any of these people can be called on to give you a reference. Choose carefully, and don't abuse a friendship if you think your friend might hesitate to comply. Always ask someone if they object before you give their name as a referee and thank them afterwards (especially if you get the job!).

If you are asked to give a reference for a friend or acquaintance, agree only if you are happy to do so, rather than being put in the position of giving a lukewarm or downright untrue reference. Be wary of giving a reference addressed 'To Whom It May Concern' rather than to a named individual. An 'open' reference may be touted round inappropriately to many different companies, when you might prefer to tailor your remarks according to the occasion.

Office etiquette It goes without saying that you'll do your job to the best of your ability. Over and above that, the most important aspect of a successful working life is to develop a sound professional relationship with your boss and close colleagues, based preferably on mutual respect. Once it is known that you can be relied on to do your work well and conscientiously, you may be able to negotiate more flexibility in the way you work, but do this gradually and not before you have demonstrated that you are on top of the job.

It's pleasant to get on well with colleagues, but advisable to keep office relationships on a purely professional, rather than social, footing, at least until you have sussed out the lie of the land. There's no such thing as an office without politics, and it pays off to be aware of these, even if you don't participate. And if you go in for a spot of wheeler-dealing yourself, that's all the more reason to stay a little aloof from too much relaxed socializing with colleagues.

Office love affairs are inadvisable at best, and can be disastrous. They are far too distracting when in full flight, and definitely too disruptive if they come to grief.

Avoid gossip and keep the in-depth details of your private life under your hat during working hours. Personal phone calls should be short and kept to the minimum. Don't be tempted to filch office stationery or postage, or fiddle expenses, even if 'everyone does it'. Every so often the most blind-eyed managements are capable of clamping down, which is so much the worse for anyone caught metaphorically with a hand in the till.

Beware of overdoing the alcohol during lunch breaks or at office parties (*see* BEING A GUEST AT WORK, page 68 and ENTERTAINING ON BUSINESS, page 85).

Remember when you answer the phone or greet clients that you are representing the company (*see also* EVERYDAY DRESS, page 106). Be friendly without overdoing it, patient, polite and helpful even in the face of provocation.

Q *I'm a solicitor, and occasionally friends who are not clients phone me to ask my advice on some legal point or other. This is often highly inconvenient, since I am generally up to my eyes in work, but how can I refuse without offending them?*

A Tell them that unfortunately you are just too busy to answer their question, which requires some research on your part. If they persist, explain that you are inundated with work, and that if their question requires more than a straight 'yes or no' answer, you will have to charge them for your time.

Q *At an interview recently I was asked if I intended to have* *any more children (my son is three). I'm sure that question is illegal these days, but I was taken so much surprised I replied: 'I don't know'. What should I have said?*

A You could have refused to answer, saying that you believed it to be unlawful to ask such a question. However, such a reply might have undermined your chances of getting the job, so the reply you gave was probably as good as any, since it didn't commit you either way.

Dealing with divorce

Divorce is a sad fact of life that few of us can choose to ignore. It takes courage to deal with it in the face of the outside world, and a tactful and sensitive attitude on the part of others helps enormously in what is inevitably a difficult situation.

When a couple separate the news usually gets around fast. If you meet someone who you know has separated recently it is polite to express your sadness, but you should not probe into the reasons (*see also* OTHER PERSONAL LETTERS, page 44). Likewise, a person who is newly separated may have to face up to unwelcome questions, and the quicker he or she can learn to deflect these with some vague remark – 'We both decided it was for the best' – the better.

It's a pity, although understandable, that friends of a separated couple sometimes decide to keep in touch with only one partner. Those who would like to continue seeing both have to tread a careful path, especially in the months immediately following the separation. Try to avoid a situation where both partners confide in you, or canvass your opinion on their ex's behaviour or current doings.

After separation/divorce What happens to jointly owned property, which generally includes the accumulated possessions of several years, can only be decided by the individuals involved. Tempting though it may be to fight over every last teaspoon, long drawn out wrangles only breed bitterness and distress. It's often better in the long run to cut your losses and make a new start.

It takes time to get used to a new status of single person. Friends can help enormously here by continuing to include the newly-single at social gatherings regardless of the fact that they have no partner, and also by offering support and help to struggling single parents.

Whether you decide to keep in touch with your ex's family will depend on the circumstances. It is often a cause of great sorrow to separate grandparents from their grandchildren and it's well worth striving to keep up some friendly contact even if it has to be fairly distant.

Remarriage *See* ETIQUETTE FOR SECOND MARRIAGES, page 122, for details of how to conduct the wedding. Once wed, another set of adjustments has to be made, by the whole extended family. If you are in touch with your ex-spouse (very likely if you have children) it makes things a lot easier if he or she is at least on speaking terms with your new partner, although the two may prefer not to meet.

There's no need to announce that this is your second spouse when making introductions. If you acquire a family of step-children you will all have to make the sometimes delicate decision of what to call each other. Very young children who have taken easily to calling a step-parent 'Mummy' or 'Daddy' can be introduced as your son or daughter if that feels natural, or as your step-son or daughter if you prefer. Older children, or those who don't live with you usually find it easier to call their step-parent by his or her Christian name or a nick name. Introduce them by saying 'This is my step-son, Tom,' if the relationship is close enough; or 'This is Tom, Mike's son.'

These may seem like trivial points, but who is called what can turn into a major issue during the early stages of adjustment in step-families. Being sensitive to each other's feelings is just the beginning of forging sound, workable relationships in a step-family, but it is an important starting point.

Q *My husband's children spend every weekend with us and we drop them back home to his ex-wife on Sunday evening. Several times she has asked him to come in to say hello to a visiting friend or relative. When this happens I am left sitting outside in the car, fuming. Am I wrong to object to this treatment?*

A No, your husband's ex is being very discourteous to expect you to wait around outside. In future, ask your husband to refuse to go in, on the grounds that you are being kept waiting or to take you inside with him, although this could be awkward. Alternatively, you could suggest that he takes the children home without you.

Q *My sister was divorced last year, having been married for 22 years. Since then, her ex-husband has died. Should she now describe herself as a widow?*

A No, because a woman only becomes a widow when the man to whom she is married dies. Your sister can say either that she is single or a divorcee.

Q *I've always had a good relationship with my ex-husband's family and still see them frequently even though I have now remarried. Strictly speaking, am I still an aunt to his nephews and nieces?*

A Technically the relationship ended when you divorced. But there's no reason why the children can't still call you 'Auntie'. If you ever need to introduce them you can say: 'This is Sophie, my former sister-in-law's daughter.'

Out and about

Staying in hotels   When you arrive at a hotel you will be asked to sign the register. These days this procedure holds no fear for unmarried couples as it did in the past. Only one person need sign.

You may be offered help to take your luggage to your room, and the porter should be given a tip of about 50p to £1 depending on the star-rating of the hotel and whether the porter is a young lad or a uniformed expert. At a top class hotel you can ring for room service at any hour of the day or night. Otherwise meals may be served at set times and you will usually find details in your room, or at reception.

Tipping   Not as prevalent as it was, but there are still occasions when a tip is very definitely expected. When leaving a hotel after a reasonably long stay you should tip the chambermaid, but this is not necessary on short business trips. If you stay at a country house where there are staff you should tip the person who makes the beds and the cook. Men should tip the butler. You can leave cash on your dressing table or with your hostess, or offer it discreetly to the individuals concerned.

At the hairdresser it is usual to give the stylist a tip of 10% plus 50p to the junior who washed your hair. It is not usual to tip the owner of the salon if he or she has done your hair.

Taxi drivers expect around 10% to be added on to the fare as you pay. In restaurants, check the bill to see if a service charge has been included. If it has there is no need to add a further tip, although too many restaurants have the habit of presenting customers with a credit slip on which the total has been left blank, presumably hoping for an additional 10% on top. When no service charge is made, you should leave 10–12½% of the total as a tip, more if the service was exceptionally good. Ask the waiter or waitress if he or she will receive the tip if you include it in the total cheque or credit card bill. It is generally better to leave the tip in cash, so that it reaches the person who gave you service. If you have been unhappy with the service received you are quite within your rights to refuse a tip, but be prepared to explain your reasons if a disagreement ensues.

Q *At a local restaurant recently we were kept waiting for 45 minutes after ordering, with no explanation or apology. When the food arrived one dish was lukewarm, the other was not what we had ordered and we had to send both back. The bill included a 12½% service charge, which we deducted from the total before writing our cheque. However, the manager then appeared and demanded that we pay the full amount. Rather than cause a scene we eventually gave him the extra money. Was there anything we could have done?*

A Although in theory you had every right to withhold the service charge given the quality of the service you had received, you were probably wise to pay up and leave rather than allow an unpleasant row to escalate. You could consider writing to the manager or to head office, if the restaurant is part of a chain, and trying to extract an apology and some compensation. Failing that, you can do no more than warn your friends off this establishment, and vow never to set foot inside again.

2

Letters and invitations

Quick and easy though it is, there are times when a phone call just won't do. Sometimes it's important to have a written record of an exchange: if you're making a complaint, for instance; arranging a complicated job; requesting or confirming a detailed estimate. At other times what has to be said is too difficult to put into spoken words. Condolences, congratulations or apologies are often easier to express in writing. And taking time to send a written thank-you when someone has gone to a lot of trouble to entertain or help you, is a thoughtful way to show your gratitude.

Addressing envelopes

Write the address clearly in the lower half of the envelope, where there's no chance of it being obscured by a wayward postmark. The postcode should be written on a line by itself, with a clear space between the two halves of the code. If you like, print your own address on the back flap of the envelope, so that the letter can easily be returned to you unopened if for any reason the Post Office cannot deliver it. Should the letter contain any material intended for the eyes of the recipient only, write 'Personal' or 'Confidential' in the top left-hand corner of the envelope and at the top of the letter.

Addressing women   Problems arise here because of the sheer number of possibilities and also because many women are rather sensitive about how they are addressed. Unfortunately, it's not simply a matter of whether a woman is married or single. She may use her married name at times and her maiden name at others; she may be quite happy with Ms but detest Miss (or vice versa); she may prefer no title at all; she may be divorced but still use her married name, or have reverted to her maiden name.

Follow the preference of the woman to whom you are writing if you know it. Otherwise you'll just have to make a choice from the various options. For an unmarried woman, address the envelope to Miss Sally Jones, Ms Sally Jones or Sally Jones. If there are several unmarried daughters living at home, the traditional convention is to address the eldest one as Miss Jones and add Christian names for the younger daughters, although to be sure of avoiding confusion it might be better to use Christian name or initials for the eldest as well. If you are writing to them all, address the envelope to The Misses Jones.

Letters to married women can be addressed to Mrs James Price or Mrs J Price. Some married women prefer to be addressed as Mrs Mary Price, a style formerly reserved for divorced women, and Ms Mary Price or Mary Price are also acceptable. When writing a business letter to a married woman, use her own Christian name or initials, and not her husband's (even if you know them). To complicate matters still further, some married women do not change their name when they marry (*see* ADDRESSING COUPLES, page 32), and others keep their maiden name at work while using their married name in private life and so must be addressed differently depending on the circumstances.

Widows can be addressed as Mrs Philip Brown or Mrs Brown. Divorced women who keep their married name can be called Mrs Mary Dove or Mrs M Dove (or Mrs Dove, Mary Dove or Ms Dove). Divorced women who revert to their maiden name also revert to the title Miss (but may prefer Ms, or no title).

What happens if you don't know a woman's marital status? The old custom was to use 'Mrs' as a courtesy, but these days that could just as easily cause offence. You can always ask, if you get the opportunity, and if not opt for Ms Sally Jones or Sally Jones. If a woman is asked 'Is that Miss or Mrs?', when she gives her name, she should take the opportunity to state her preference, saying if necessary 'I prefer Ms', or 'Just use Sally Jones'.

With such a plethora of choice there is inevitably a small risk of causing offence whatever title you choose. In the end, however, a woman can only blame herself if she doesn't make it clear what form of address she prefers (*see* ENDING A LETTER, page 35) and shouldn't feel slighted if someone has selected the wrong title in an attempt to be courteous.

Addressing men Men are much easier. Choose from Mr James Price, James Price, or James Price Esq. 'Esq', short for Esquire, has a more formal and old-fashioned ring about it and was formerly used by the 'professional' classes to differentiate between themselves and tradespeople. Nowadays, of course, no such distinctions are made and many people use 'Mr' for all correspondence. Master James Price is bordering on the quaint, but can be used for little boys. Otherwise use James Price for children and young teenagers.

Addressing couples Mr and Mrs James Price; Mr and Mrs Price or James and Sally Price are all fine for married couples. If the couple occupy the same address but are unmarried, or if the wife has not taken her husband's name, address them as James Price and Sally Jones.

Other forms of address Now and then you may need to write to a doctor, clergyman, your local MP or someone else who doesn't fit into the day-to-day categories.

Clergy Envelope: The Reverend Michael Connor. Letter begins Dear Mr Connor or Dear Father Connor.

Doctors Envelope: Susan Ford MD, or Dr Susan Ford; Andrew White [Esq] MD or Dr Andrew White. Letter begins Dear Dr Ford or Dear Doctor.

Local Councillors Envelope: Councillor Mr John Beckley; Councillor Mrs Jane Young. Letter begins Dear Councillor.

Members of Parliament Envelope: Malcolm Burns Esq MP; Mrs Jenny Adams MP. If you are writing to an MP whom you know is also a Privy Councillor, address the envelope to The Rt Hon Malcolm Burns MP. In either case, the letter begins Dear Sir or Dear Mr Burns.

Surgeons Envelope: Mr Derek Robins, MS, FRCS. Letter begins Dear Mr Robins.

Q *As secretary of a local charitable organisation I've been asked to write to the owner of a nearby stately home, whom I believe is a Duke, to ask if he will open a fair which we plan to hold in the village. What is the correct way to address him?*

A Address the envelope to The Duke of Wherever and start the letter Dear Duke, or Dear Duke of Wherever. The whole business of addressing titled people and royalty can be very complicated. You can find full details, covering every title imaginable from Archbishop to Irish Chieftain, in *Debrett's Correct Form*, which should be available at your local reference library.

Q *On holiday in Sweden last year we made friends with a Swedish family and now I would like to write and ask them to visit us. What is the Swedish equivalent of Mr and Mrs?*

A The direct translation of Mr and Mrs is Herr och Fru. However, when writing to acquaintances abroad it is sometimes simpler to use the British titles Mr and Mrs. Other countries have all sorts of idiosyncracies of address, for instance the custom in some places of extending the husband's title, such as Doctor or Engineer, to include the wife as well (eg in Germany Dr Smith's wife is addressed as Frau Doktor Schmitt).

Writing letters

Always write your own address clearly at the top of a letter, if it is not already printed on the notepaper, even if you know your correspondent well. It saves him or her the trouble of looking it up or relying on memory. Addresses are easily forgotten or mistaken and a small slip in the postcode or house number may mean that the reply never reaches you.

The colour of paper is up to you and although white, cream or pale blue are standard, there's a whole spectrum of other colours available. It is sometimes difficult to read writing on dark coloured paper, so it's probably better to go for a paler shade. You can write on both sides of the paper or just one, as you prefer, and continue to a second, unheaded sheet if necessary. Short notes can be quickly written on postcards and you can have your name and address printed along the top of plain cards. Alternatively little sticky labels printed with your name, address and phone number are useful for sticking on to cards and brief notes where it's not worth using a sheet of headed paper.

Type your business letters, particularly if they are longer than a few sentences, and always if your handwriting verges on the illegible. Personal letters, including condolences and thanks, should be handwritten, but make sure they can be read without too much head-scratching. If your writing is totally incomprehensible even when you try hard, then it's kinder to type personal letters, but do say why and add a beginning and ending in your own hand.

It's a sensible precaution to put the recipient's name and address at the beginning of your letter when you're writing to a company. The letter may be opened at a central point and make its way to the recipient minus envelope, so it is important that the letter itself shows the name of the person for whom it is intended.

Beginning a letter Follow the style used on the envelope: Dear Mr Price, Dear Miss/Mrs/Ms Jones. Dear Sally Jones or Dear James Price are generally acceptable and useful if you don't know a woman's title, or want to strike a level of informality without using a Christian name on its own.

Address someone as Dear James only if you have already established that the two of you are on Christian name terms. If you write to someone as Dear Mr Price or Dear James Price, and his reply comes back signed 'James', take that as your signal to start your next letter Dear James.

When writing to a nameless face within an organization you can start the letter Dear Sir, Dear Madam or Dear Sir or Madam. To be less formal and friendlier you could use the name of the company or department instead: Dear Telford Flooring; Dear Rentals Department. As so often occurs with etiquette, it's all a matter of personal style and preference.

Ending a letter The old rule still applies: letters beginning Dear Sir end Yours faithfully; letters beginning Dear Miss Jones or Dear Sally end Yours sincerely. As you get to know your correspondent better you could branch out into something a bit warmer: Yours; Yours ever; Yours as ever, or as always. If none of these seems quite right, you could end the letter Best wishes or With all good wishes plus your signature. If in doubt, be guided by the tone of the your correspondent's replies.

Letters to friends or family can end with whatever terms of affection you like, but it's as well to be a little circumspect about signing yourself with love to someone of the opposite sex whom you don't know closely.

It is helpful to people who don't know you well to type your name (or print it legibly in a handwritten letter) beneath your signature. This saves your correspondent having to puzzle over who the letter is from and also gives a woman the opportunity to indicate her preferred title, either before her name, or in brackets after it: Ms Sally Jones; Sally Jones (Mrs).

Q *When I write a letter from both myself and my husband, should I get him to add his signature, or sign his name myself alongside my own?*

A When either partner writes a letter which is intended

35

to come from both, the neatest way round the question of who signs is to start the letter 'James [or Margaret] and I want to thank you...'. The letter can then be signed by the writer alone.

How to write a letter

Decide what you want to say before you start writing. When you are writing a complicated letter it helps to jot down a list of points you want to cover first, in the order in which you want to raise them. Look up any information you need before you settle down at the typewriter or to pen and paper. There's no need to be curt, but don't waste time and space going over details which are already known to you and your correspondent. Stick to the point, but make sure you give enough background information to make the letter comprehensible.

Work out what result you want your letter to have. Make specific requests, whether for an estimate by a particular date, a refund, or simply a speedy reply. Decide on an appropriate tone for the letter, which may be formal, friendly but fairly distant, or very warm and informal. Be polite without grovelling or using undue flattery. By all means be witty if that's your style, but don't overdo it or you may alienate your recipient. There's no point in getting very angry in a letter, or sending someone a string of clever insults. Even if it makes you feel better, it's likely to be counter-productive, so vent your wrath among family or friends first, and compose your letter once you've had a chance to calm down.

Reply to letters promptly. And read through the letter to which you are replying to make sure you do answer all the points it raises. This applies just as much to personal letters as to business correspondence. A friend or relative who sends you a letter brimming with questions will be irritated to receive a reply which leaves every last one unanswered.

Business letters   A necessary evil and often tedious to compose, it's worth making an effort to get these right. A good letter can produce swift results, where a bad one may inspire such inertia in the recipient that it languishes unanswered for weeks. Whether you're writing to the gas board, the tax office, a local tradesman, solicitor, bank manager, shop or builder it's always better to direct your letter to a named individual. With a bit of luck one phone call will establish the best person to deal with your letter, and mean that it should land on the right desk straight away, instead of doing the rounds of other in-trays first.

Remember to date all letters and keep a copy. Quote reference numbers or account numbers every time. Follow letters up with a phone call if you haven't had a reply after a reasonable interval (although your idea of what's reasonable may not tally with that of the recipient).

Be polite and precise and don't fall into the trap of using jargon apart from specialized vocabulary. Express yourself in clear, everyday language and you eliminate the risk of misunderstandings and ensure that your message is instantly understood.

27 The Broads, Cleveham, Dorset, DS3 6KD
Tel: 0987 63245

Miss Anderson
Better Building Co
Brimblecombe
Dorset DS1 2JY

19 September 1988

Dear Miss Anderson
Job No: 1234567890
We spoke on the phone this afternoon about the delays in the work your firm has been doing at my home. Please confirm that the materials needed to finish the job will be available by 30 September, and that the work will be completed within a week from that date. Thank you.

Yours sincerely

Jane Walker (Mrs)

37

The above letter is short and to the point. It gives all the relevant information, requests a reply and is polite but businesslike.

Letters of complaint   Make sure you are legally entitled to receive whatever redress you are seeking. Examine the terms of guarantees etc before writing, but bear in mind that the law may make provision for additional redress, on top of a manufacturer's guarantee. To make a convincing complaint, it helps enormously to have a working knowledge of your rights under consumer law. Many of these are covered by the Sale of Goods Act 1979, which covers the purchase of second-hand goods as well as new, and lays down many rules to protect the consumer. Your local library should be able to provide a copy of the Act (or helpful books on consumer law) and the Citizens Advice Bureau publish leaflets on Codes of Practice governing a variety of trade organizations.

Once armed with your background information, find out the name of the appropriate person to write to by ringing the company involved. It sometimes pays off to go straight to the top with a complaint. State the facts of the case, explain why you are complaining and what you would like to be done. Give specific details of when and where the goods were bought, dates of any previous letters etc. Be sure to keep a copy of any letter you write.

If, as in the example above, the firm has offered a solution such as extending the finishing date, or removing the faulty goods, state whether or not you are prepared to accept their suggestion and if not, say what course of action you would prefer. Express your disappointment and explain how you have been inconvenienced, but don't give way to unbridled fury. Apart from anything else, if your first letter doesn't produce a response, you may need to save the big guns for a second letter. Don't threaten legal action unless you are prepared to go through with it and are sure you have a good case, as you'll lose all credibility and any chance of getting satisfaction if the firm calls your bluff.

27 The Broads, Cleveham, Dorset, DS3 6KD
Tel: 0987 63245

Mr J D Sellots
Managing Director
Glittermore Jewellery Ltd
Basingstoke
Hants
HD6 8TY

19 September 1988

Dear Mr Sellots

I bought a watch, carrying a one-month guarantee, from your Brimble-combe branch on 17 August. On 14 September I noticed that the date-change mechanism was not working, but I was unable to return the watch until 18 September as I live some distance from Brimblecombe. Your manager told me that he could do nothing as the watch was no longer under guarantee, and offered to send it to the repairer, for which I would be charged. He refused to accept my point that the watch had stopped functioning before the guarantee expired.

I was disappointed by your manager's unhelpful attitude, particular-ly as I had made a special journey into town to return the watch. Since the date was stuck on 10 September, there was no question of the watch having broken down outside the guarantee period, and in the circumst-ances I would like to be provided with a replacement as soon as possible.

Yours sincerely

Jane Walker (Mrs)

The writer must have been livid – her watch had packed up within weeks of buying it, she'd had to go all the way to town to exchange it and then the manager had insisted on sticking to the letter of the guarantee. But although her annoyance comes across in the letter, the overall tone is restrained and reasonable. She states the facts clearly and asks directly for what she wants.

Q *My new washing machine flooded my kitchen the first time I used it. I went back to the shop and asked for a refund, but they said that I would have to accept a credit note or allow their engineer to fix the machine. I wasn't happy with either of these suggestions, but the sales manager refused to offer any other solution. What do I do now?*

A You do not have to accept either of the store's suggestions, and can insist on a full refund, since the shop has broken a condition of the Sale of Goods Act 1979 by selling you faulty goods. It is unfortunate that in this case the goods are too large for you to take them back to the shop and as you have got nowhere by talking to the manager, your next step is to write to him, saying in your letter that you reject the goods as being faulty and are seeking a complete repayment. If this doesn't get you anywhere, you will have no alternative but to take the shop to court.

Thank-you letters If you've ever sent a carefully chosen gift, or held a dinner party, you'll know how much pleasure it gives to receive a written thank-you. It goes without saying that people should always be thanked promptly for generosity or hospitality. Making a phone call is often all that's necessary between close friends or family, but if the occasion was something special it's a nice gesture to send a card or note to say thanks. And for people you know less well, or see infrequently, a written thank-you is essential. Probably the hardest thank-yous to write are those for evenings of excruciating boredom, or hideous gifts. In these circumstances, keep it fairly brief and take refuge in ambiguity without being downright dishonest (*see* LITTLE WHITE LIES, page 15).

Whatever the occasion, there's no need to write reams. A

shortish letter is fine, as long as it sounds sincere and is interesting to read. No one will be thrilled with a formula bread-and-butter letter, so bring in a personal note by mentioning something specific: a dish you particularly enjoyed, someone interesting that you met, an attractive or useful aspect of the gift you've received. Aim to make the person you are thanking feel that their efforts were fully appreciated.

Postcards, either plain or with a picture, come into their own for sending thanks for an evening's hospitality or a small gift, and are especially suitable for friends. If you have been a guest overnight or longer, been entertained by people who are not close friends or received a larger gift then a short letter is more appropriate. It's not necessary to reply to a thank-you letter, although it's polite to thank the sender for writing next time you see or speak to him or her.

Thank-you letter for a dinner party:

Thank you so much for a marvellous dinner party. The whole atmosphere of the evening was lovely, and we did enjoy meeting the Morgans. It was fascinating to talk to someone who has actually lived abroad, now that we're thinking of upping sticks ourselves for a while. And what delicious food! The mango sorbet was superb; the perfect dish to round off an excellent meal.
Good company, good food – there's nothing better! Thanks again for a truly memorable evening.

After a wedding, engagement party or housewarming, when many gifts have been received, try and find time to write individually to everyone, rather than sending printed 'Thank-you' cards. Most people go to a lot of trouble to choose a present that will be liked, and are very pleased to receive a personal thank-you, even if it arrives up to a month after the big event.

Thank-you letter for a wedding present:

Thank you very much for the casserole you sent us as a wedding present. It's the perfect size for two and you couldn't have picked a better colour than that lovely cheerful red, which looks great in our new grey and white kitchen. We've given it pride of place in one of our glass-fronted cupboards, so it's on full view. It's already been much admired and is in regular use on these chilly evenings.

We have been back from honeymoon for a week now, and the wedding seems like a lifetime ago because there's been so much to do in the house. The kitchen was finished while we were away, and we've embarked on the living room. It's all a bit chaotic at the moment, but once we're sorted out you must come over and see our handiwork. Until then, thanks again from both of us for such a thoughtful present, which will give us pleasure both to use and to look at for years to come.

Letters of condolence   Most people find these the hardest of all to write. Don't give up though, no matter how daunting the task of finding the right words. People who have been bereaved often find immense comfort in the thoughtful and caring letters they receive at a time when life seems so bleak.

Letters can differ in length and intimacy depending on how well you knew the person who has died. For a neighbour or acquaintance it's enough just to write briefly to express your sadness at the news and extend your sympathy to the person who has been bereaved. If appropriate you can offer practical help. However, if you knew the person who has died reasonably well you can also add a paragraph or two about your pleasant memories of them.

Write letters of condolence immediately you hear the news (unless, of course, the family place a newspaper advertisement of the funeral specifying 'no letters').

Letter to the widow of a colleague:

I was so sorry to hear of John's death last week. He and I worked together for many years and I always found his judgement sound and his sense of humour delightful. It was a pleasure to go to meetings chaired by John because of his knack of getting straight to the point, and he was much respected in the organization. We will miss him very much. He often spoke of you and the children, and his family was obviously a very important source of happiness in his life.

Please accept my deepest sympathy.

Letter to a close friend on the death of his wife:

We were shocked and greatly saddened to hear of Hannah's sudden death, and we wanted you to know that we are thinking of you at this terrible time.

Words seem inadequate when someone we all loved so much dies. Hannah was a wonderful friend and it has been a privilege and a joy to share in her enthusiasm, wit and warmth over all the years we have known you both. We will always remember her laughter on all those happy evenings we spent with you, her superb cooking and generous hospitality, her pride in her beautiful garden and her talent for drawing people out and making friends. She was a remarkable person of many exceptional qualities, and our lives have been enriched by knowing her.

Our hearts and thoughts are with you. If there is anything at all we can do to help, you have only to tell us.

Letters of condolence should receive a reply as soon after the funeral as possible. The reply can be short and the same basic wording, with a few variations, can probably be used to answer most letters. Anyone who sent flowers should also be thanked. Another member of the family can write on behalf of the widow or widower, saying 'My mother/father has asked me to write...'. If there are a great many letters and replying will take several weeks you can place an interim advertisement in the personal column of a national newspaper, thanking people for their sympathy.

Reply to letter of condolence:

Thank you very much for your kind letter at the time of John's death. Over the last few weeks, as I begin to pick up the pieces of my life, it has been a great comfort to hear how much my husband meant to others and how greatly he will be missed. He often talked about his colleagues at Truby Brothers and I know he was very proud to be involved with such an excellent team of people.
Thank you again for your thoughtfulness.

Other personal letters There are many times when a phone call or card doesn't seem enough, or when what you want to say is too tricky to tackle face to face. For instance, you might want to apologise because you fear someone has been offended, or to tell a friend that you are sorry to hear of some misfortune such as an accident, divorce, or job loss.

These sort of letters are best kept brief – say too much and you run the risk of writing yourself into a corner. Try to sound sincere. Don't apologise fulsomely if the occasion doesn't warrant it, say instead that you are sorry for whatever has happened (without apportioning blame or going through the ins and outs of the whole affair all over again) and you hope the friendship won't be affected in future.

When you're writing to offer sympathy say how sad you were to hear of whatever has happened and offer help if appropriate. If you write to a newly divorced friend, don't take sides, and don't make assumptions about why the marriage has ended or write anything that you might regret later about either party. There's no reason at all why you can't write to both partners and keep in touch with them separately.

Letter to a newly divorced friend:

We were so sorry to hear of your recent divorce. You must have been through a thoroughly distressing time and be feeling very unsettled – do let us know if there is anything we can do to help. It is always sad when a marriage breaks up, whatever the reason, but we wanted you to know that you can still count on our friendship, so please don't hesitate to ring us if you need any practical help or just a chat.

A letter like this does the groundwork of renewing contact after an event such as a divorce, and can be followed up with a phone call a few days later.

On a happier note you might want to send congratulations on the birth of a baby, an important exam passed, a promotion or honour. Again, aim for sincerity and don't be afraid to let your feelings show if you're delighted. The letter will read all the better for a spot of real enthusiasm.

Letter of congratulations:

Congratulations! I've just heard that you're now a fully-fledged BA of the Open University. I'm so glad that those years of sheer hard slog have paid off. You must be thrilled that at long last you can write BA after your name and have a few well-earned lie-ins. Getting up at 6am to study can't have been much fun and I really admire the way you've stuck at it – such determination deserves to be rewarded. Let's meet up while you've got some spare time. We'd better make it soon, because knowing you you'll be starting an MA course any minute now, so I'll give you a ring next week to fix a date. Once again, well done.

Q *A close friend has sent me a birthday present in the post every year for the last ten years, but this year nothing arrived. Should I send her a present on her birthday as usual?*

A As your exchange of gifts has gone on uninterrupted for so many years, and you don't mention anything that has happened to cause a rift between you, it does seem very unlikely that she would just stop sending a present without saying anything. Much more likely is that the parcel is lost in the post, and she is wondering why you haven't thanked her for it. Ring or write to her quickly to clear the matter up. And go ahead and send her a gift as usual.

Q *I find the whole business of letter writing terribly difficult. I agonize for hours over the right wording and find when I've finished that the letter often sounds false.*

A You're spending so long pondering over every word that the letter loses any spontaneity. Don't worry so much about the impression you're creating. It's much better to write straight from the heart and not bother if one or two sentences aren't models of perfect grammar. Next time you write a letter, once you're reasonably happy with it, leave it overnight and read it through again next day. Taking a break like this makes it easier to spot any bad style or errors. Another tip is to read it out loud to yourself, or get someone else to read it to you. That way you'll soon find the places that sound stilted or unnatural.

Invitations

Formal invitations   These are always sent for weddings, and sometimes for large parties. You can have cards specially printed, and the printer will have examples of different styles and wording. The standard wording for a wedding invitation is:

Mr and Mrs Richard Marsden
request the pleasure of the company of
Mr and Mrs Alec Wilson
at the marriage of their daughter
Sarah Suzanne
with
Mr Christopher Malcolm Hill
at St Justin's Parish Church, Brimblecombe
on Saturday 10 June 19 . . . at 2.30pm
and afterwards at the Old Bull Hotel, Brimblecombe

RSVP: 17 Cleveland Avenue
Brimblecombe, Dorset DS1 5TZ

See pages 136–8 for further examples. Examples of other wordings to use in different family circumstances, for instance if the bride's parents are divorced or for a second marriage are given in the section on Weddings, pages 119–20.

Formal invitations to other events follow similar lines:

Mr and Mrs David Walker
request the pleasure of Miss Judith Holland's company on
Friday 19 April 19 . . . at 7.00pm

DRINKS

RSVP: 27 The Broads
Cleveham
Dorset DS3 6KD

Replying to formal invitations   Strictly speaking, you should reply formally in the same style of wording as the invitation. Use headed notepaper and don't add a signature. Mention the names of all the hosts in your reply and also on the envelope, which should be sent to the address given on the invitation.

Mr and Mrs Alec Wilson thank Mr and Mrs Marsden for their kind invitation to the wedding of their daughter Sarah on Saturday 10 June, and have great pleasure in accepting

or

and much regret that they will be unable to attend as they have a previous engagement.

If you have to refuse a formal invitation this can be done using the wording shown above, but it is more courteous to send your regrets and a brief explanation in a letter.

Thank you very much for inviting us to Sarah's wedding. I'm afraid that much as we would love to join you, the date coincides with the arrival of Alec's mother from Canada, and so 2.30 will find us en route for the airport. I do hope the celebrations go well, and you can be sure that we will raise a glass to you all that evening! Please pass on our love to Sarah and Christopher and our best wishes for their big day.

If a formal invitation comes from friends it is perfectly acceptable to write a short, informal letter in reply rather than using the formal wording.

Thank you for your invitation to Drinks on Friday 19th. I'd be delighted to come and am looking forward to seeing you both again.

Informal invitations   Invites to dinner parties, casual drinks parties and most other occasions can be sent as an informal note or card, or given over the phone. You can invite people from about ten days to three weeks before the event, although closer friends can be given shorter notice.

The advantage of phoning is that you get a definite yes or no straight away. Writing RSVP on invitations will provoke some response, but you may have to do some follow-up work on the phone the week before your party to get a final idea of numbers.

There are several things people need to know when they receive an invitation, whether written or verbal: the occasion (is it a birthday or special celebration?); the date and address; when to arrive and when to leave; how large a party it is; what should they wear; should they bring a bottle (or even some food); can they bring a partner? Include a map or written directions if your home is hard to find.

Replying to informal invitations   You can telephone a reply to a written invitation or drop your host/ess a note. Whichever you do, do it promptly. Using the phone gives you a chance to find out more if the invitation has not covered every detail: 'Is it a big party?', 'Are you dressing up?' If you can't attend you must give a good reason, even if in truth you just don't want to go.

Q *I took my boyfriend along to a party even though the invitation only mentioned my name, because I thought it was going to be a large gathering and one more person wouldn't make any difference. When we arrived I realized that it was actually a small dinner party and it was obvious that he was not expected. It was all very embarrassing, even though our hosts smoothed things over. What should I have done?*

A Regardless of how big a party is you should always ask before taking along another guest. If you'd rung your hosts as soon as you received the invitation and saw that your boyfriend's name was not mentioned, you could have found out that it was a smaller party than you'd imagined, and asked if they minded one extra guest. However, it would have been thoughtful of your hosts to have made it clear that the invitation was to a small party and also to ask you whether you would like to bring an escort.

3

Introductions and meetings

Very few people, even those who appear totally confident, feel instantly at ease in a group of strangers. The first few minutes at a party as guests cast around anxiously looking for a friendly face, can be particularly daunting. Hosts owe it to their guests to make introductions promptly so that they can quickly get into the swing of things.

Introductions

Convention dictates that men are introduced to women ('James Price, meet Sally Jones'). Convention also reckons that younger people should be introduced to older, and those of junior 'rank' to their seniors. That's all very well when such distinctions are obvious. Frequently they are not, in which case no one is likely to care much who is introduced to whom provided both names are pronounced clearly when the introduction is made.

The two being introduced should make eye contact, shake hands or nod to each other and say 'how do you do', or 'hello'.

Again, the 'rules' say that men should stand up when being introduced to a woman, while women can remain seated when introductions are made. However, if there's a general uprising as newcomers arrive, women may feel more comfortable if they stand too. And it's a polite gesture for them to do so when meeting someone much older.

At a large gathering, where the host can make only brief introductions before he or she leaves guests to fend for themselves, it is helpful to add a fact or two to the introduction to give people a reference point from which to start the conversational ball rolling. 'James, this is Sally Jones who has just moved in across the road. Sally, James Price. James has just finished having some work done on his house, so I'm sure he can advise you about local builders.'

When to use Christian names Introduce people to each other by their full names, eg Margaret Stevens. Most people will automatically start to use Christian names as they talk. If using a Christian name feels uncomfortable – when you meet someone older, or a senior colleague, for instance – say 'Mrs Stevens' until she invites you to: 'Please call me Margaret'.

Remembering names It's extraordinary how names disappear into the recesses of the memory just when they are needed most.

If you're making the introductions, familiarize yourself with the names of all guests (and their partners) before the party. Should your mind go an appalling blank at the crucial moment you can either take the coward's way out and disappear, saying 'I'll leave you to introduce yourselves,' or laugh apologetically, confess to your momentary lapse and beg for help. Few people will be hurt by your forgetfulness, since most have found themselves in the same dilemma at some time or other.

When you're on the receiving end of an introduction, or worse, a string of introductions, be prepared. Fight hard not to glaze over. Listen to the names, and use the old trick of repeating the other person's name as you greet them: 'How do you do, Sally.' Another aide-memoire that can be surprisingly effective is to make a private mental link between the person's name and something about their appearance (Glynis: glasses; Peter: paunch).

What's in a name? Suppose that when you are introduced your host makes a slip over your name, or the other person immediately shortens your name or starts using the wrong one. There's nothing for it, but to take a deep breath and point the mistake out straight away. 'Actually it's *Sally* Jones, not Sarah', 'By the way, I'm usually called Elizabeth rather than Liz.' Do it pleasantly, but do it, even if you feel slightly embarrassed. The potential for embarrassment is far greater if the mistake is allowed to continue uncorrected. If the direct approach is just too difficult you could try being more subtle, and working your name into an anecdote: 'When I asked my boss if I could leave work a bit early to come here, he said Oh Sarah, that's the third party you've been to this week, and it's only Tuesday!'

Assorted introductions When you are introducing your friend or partner to others, there's no need to go into any details about your own relationship. Whether your companion is your live-in lover, new boy/girlfriend or merely an acquaintance is no one else's business, and you can just say 'This is Alan Preston' and leave it at that. Likewise, when you introduce an unmarried couple to others, say 'This is Alan Preston and Suzie Mayhew.'

Women sometimes use a professional name which is different from their married name. While some stick to their professional names at all times, others adopt their married identity outside office hours. If you don't know which persona will be worn to your party, the only answer is to make enquiries beforehand.

When children are present at a gathering of adults they should be introduced: 'This is my son Edward – Sally Jones.' Whether Edward then calls your friend 'Sally' or 'Miss Jones' depends on the usual levels of formality that apply in your household.

If you arrive at a party to find no hosts in sight and a sea of unfamiliar faces, you've no choice but to dive in. Find someone else who is alone, introduce yourself and make some remark about the party to start the conversation. If as a guest you see a newcomer hovering uncertainly by the door, take the initiative to go up and chat to them.

Q *I've never met my boss's husband, although we have spoken on the phone once or twice. However, recently he was at a formal luncheon which I attended. Should I have gone over and introduced myself?*

A Yes, it would have been a good opportunity to meet him properly, especially since you have already talked to each other.

Q *When I got married I kept my maiden name, but now that I am expecting my first baby I would like to start using the same surname as my husband. How should I let people know about this?*

A Decide whether you want to be known as Anna Matthews or Mrs Simon Matthews. Tell close friends and family either in person, or by dropping them a brief note. Notify less personal connections with a card stating: 'Anna Simmonds requests that in future all correspondence be addressed to Anna Matthews.'

Q *I've been a widow for two years, and I've recently started going out with a man. I'd like him to meet my late husband's family next time they visit, but what should I say when I introduce him?*

A There's no need to offer any explanations. Just say 'I'd like you to meet my friend John Briggs'.

Well met

When you are out with a friend and meet someone else that you know in the street, it's thoughtful to introduce them to each other. Don't stop and chat for too long so that your companion has to stand around feeling out of it, or wanders off.

The art of the social kiss In many parts of the country the kiss on greeting (and leaving) is more commonplace than the handshake, even among people who don't know each other particularly well. If a cheek is proffered you should certainly not hesitate to peck it. Some people go for the double kiss, or even the triple. To avoid an unseemly clash, aim to touch left cheeks first.

Time to leave See above: you may find you shake hands with a stranger at the start of the evening, but part with a kiss by the end. It all depends on the mood of the occasion and if everyone has had a jolly time there could well be kisses all round. Otherwise, you can shake hands with individuals when you leave, or say goodbye individually, using people's names (if you remember them!). At a large party, a blanket 'goodbye' and wave to the assembled throng may be enough. But you should always seek out and thank your host personally before leaving.

If you've got on well with someone and part with the ubiquitous 'We must have lunch', by all means show enthusiasm and even offer your phone number. But don't try and fix a date there and then. They'll take the trouble to contact you if they really want to.

Q *I was out with a friend when we bumped into the local vicar. We stopped to talk for a couple of minutes, and I noticed that she called him 'Vicar'. In the past I've always called him 'Mr Cullen', but now I wonder whether I was wrong?*

A Neither is wrong, and you can use whichever form of address you prefer.

Making conversation

In an ideal world, conversation is stimulating, enjoyable and flows naturally. Some people seem to have no trouble at all in keeping a conversation going, no matter what company they find themselves in. They can stop reading now.

Others, whether shy, self-conscious or just inexperienced, find the whole business of talking to people they hardly know thoroughly alarming. Once the introductions are over they are in danger of becoming tongue-tied and panicky.

Making conversation is a skill that can be learned and needs practice. The first thing to remember if you feel shy about opening your mouth is that the majority of people also feel a bit nervous with strangers and will be thankful to you for starting to talk. Remind yourself that your thoughts and opinions are just as valid as anyone else's. People as a rule are tolerant, and there's little need to worry about making a fool of yourself.

Take comfort too in the thought that if you find a particular person hard-going, it could be because *they* have a problem talking to others, rather than you.

When you know that an event where you'll be talking to people is coming up, try and find out something about the other guests in advance. This will give you useful clues as to the things they might like to talk about. A good start to a conversation is an enquiry about a person's job, children or holiday plans. Yes, these are well-worn subjects, but they are also universal preoccupations which loom large in many people's lives. With luck, once you've started on one of these, it will lead on to other topics. Don't be afraid of asking questions; it's not nosy to be curious about another person's life. Good conversation can only happen when both parties are genuinely interested in what the other has to say.

It's true that most people will talk about themselves without much prompting. However, it is frustrating for the listener to sit through an incessant monologue without getting a chance to express his or her own views. If you realise that someone is drawing you out with questions, try to turn the tables after a while and give them a chance to talk. In that way you'll both come away from the conversation feeling satisfied.

Making good conversation does not depend on having an encyclopedic knowledge of current affairs or the arts, or a sparkling wit. It's much more useful to know a bit about a lot of topics and you can glean plenty of material from everyday sources such as books, newspapers, magazines, tv and radio. Get into the habit of mentally noting items that interest or intrigue you, so that you can air them in conversation later on.

If you are shy, try and contribute something to the general conversation early on. The longer you leave it the more tongue-tied you will get and the more likely others are to notice that you aren't saying anything. If your partner is naturally more talkative than you, enlist his or her discreet help in making openings, or asking for your opinion so that you get a chance to speak. Once you've spoken a couple of times you'll feel less inhibited.

Topics to avoid There's no need to stay off politics and religion these days, as there once was, and in fact these subjects are often likely to be discussed. Beware though of getting on to a hobby-horse and boring the rest of the company to tears. Not everyone finds these topics particularly fascinating.

The only proviso when the conversation turns to potentially controversial subjects is that the host should keep an ear open to make sure that the talk isn't likely to offend or distress anyone present who would be tentative about standing up for themselves.

Although there are few real taboos it's sensible to exercise caution when talking about money or age, as these are areas where people can be hypersensitive. Also, if you don't know the others well, avoid making assumptions about their relationships with each other.

Troubleshooting If someone makes a real gaffe, it's up to the host to smooth things over and change the subject as unobtrusively as possible. How this is done depends on the circumstances, and sometimes there's nothing that can be said to retrieve the situation. It may be appropriate to turn the remark into a joke, or to carry on and ignore it.

Should two people get into a real argument – as opposed to a heated discussion – again a third party, usually the host, must step in. Witnessing a full-scale row is embarrassing and tedious for everyone else, and if subtle attempts to lower the temperature don't work, you may have to say smilingly 'I think it's time we changed the subject before you two come to blows,' and then start another topic.

Occasionally most of us meet someone we can't stand.

When this happens, grit your teeth and put on a brave face. Don't be icy, and try not to show open hostility or boredom. It creates an unpleasant atmosphere, no matter how justified, and you'll be doing everyone a favour if you can contain your feelings until you get home.

Silence occasionally falls even at lively parties. When it happens, then someone has to take the initiative quickly and throw a question into the air – what it is hardly matters – to get the conversation going again.

Q *At a party recently, a man I did not know said something very unpleasant to the group at large about a close friend of mine. What he said was untrue, but it was seized on by others there, who went on to talk about my friend rather bitchily for a few minutes before the conversation moved on to something else. I fumed silently while all this was going on. What should I have done?*

A As soon as the initial remark was made you should have said: 'Before you go on, I think you should know that Vicky is one of my closest friends.' That would have stopped the line of conversation before it got out of hand, when it would have been far more difficult to announce your interest.

Q *We were invited to a party given by some neighbours and among the guests was a well-known politician who also lives locally. I felt rather overawed by her and avoided talking to her, partly because I didn't know what to say. Afterwards I kicked myself for having missed an interesting opportunity.*

A If you meet someone famous there's no need to pretend that they are not well-known, and it's quite all right to ask them about their achievements and experiences. In your case, you could also have talked to the politician as to any other neighbour, and discussed matters of local interest.

Telephone etiquette

When you ring a friend for a chat ask if it's a convenient moment before you launch into your news. If a friend rings you and chatters on obliviously when you want to get away, say: 'I'm sorry, I can't talk any longer now. Can I ring you back [suggest a time]?' But do ring back when you said you would.

Phone calls can often catch people off guard, and if someone rings to ask a favour, remember you don't have to say yes or no on the spot. You can always say you'll think about it and ring back later – but make sure you do. Don't be coerced into saying yes if you really want to refuse. Saying no is always difficult, but with practice it is possible to get the knack of doing it pleasantly.

A sensible precaution for women is to answer the phone with 'Hello' only, not giving number or name. Women who live alone should be listed in the phone book under initial and surname only, or go ex-directory.

The practice of selling anything from double glazing to kitchens through unsolicited phone calls is becoming widespread. It's tempting just to hang up on these callers, but if that goes too much against the grain, try saying: 'I'm not interested in buying any goods over the phone thank you' or even 'I object to this method of selling, so please remove me from your list' before ringing off.

Answerphones The style of outgoing announcement depends on personal choice. Women should be wary about stating their name or number as this might encourage nuisance callers to ring back later, or even to leave an unpleasant message.

When recording your announcement speak clearly but not ponderously. Don't gabble either, and repeat any vital details, such as another number where you can be reached.

Bear in mind security and don't announce dates when you are going to be away on business or holiday. Machines which allow you to ring in from another telephone and collect your messages are useful, because you can return calls without callers being aware that you have not been home to collect the messages.

Keep your outgoing announcement short and concise. A simple announcement might say: 'This is [if you decide to give name or number]. I can't answer your call at the moment, but please leave a message after the tone and I'll ring you back as soon as I can.'

Try ringing your machine from another number to judge the effect, or get a friend to give you an honest opinion. It's easy to come across sounding abrupt and unfriendly, and this is very offputting for callers. To get over this problem, try smiling as you record the message. You'll feel a fool as you do it, but your voice will come across with more warmth on the tape.

When a machine answers your call, hang up only if you need time to compose a suitable message. There's nothing more infuriating for answering machine owners than to find a trail of dialling tones on the tape when they come home, and no messages. When you do leave a message, make it brief. Some machines cut off automatically after 30 seconds. Speak clearly, especially if you are leaving information such as a phone number, and slowly enough so the recipient can write the information down as it plays back. Don't forget to say who you are: answering machines can distort the voice and to receive a message from a disembodied person identified only as 'it's me' is not helpful. It can be useful to give the time of your message, and even the date if you suspect the person you are calling may be away.

Q *Should I offer to pay if I need to make a phone call from a friends house? If so, how can I work out how much to give?*

A Try and avoid making phone calls from someone else's home and if you have to – to ring someone at home and ask them to pick you up, for instance – ask if you can make a quick phone call and keep it very brief.

Most people won't object or expect payment, so you need only say thanks. If you ever have to make a long distance call, while staying with friends for instance, make the call through the operator and ask for ADC (advise duration and charge). When the call is completed the operator will ring you back and tell you how much it cost so that you can offer your hosts appropriate payment.

4

The perfect guest

Cultivate the art of being a welcome, trouble-free guest and you'll never be short of invitations. It's worth doing because being entertained is fun. You have none of the work or worry, nor do you have to spend much money. All you do is enjoy yourself.

It makes a lot of sense therefore to avoid the traps that could label you as a bad guest, for most hosts will close the door after these have left with a sigh of relief, vowing 'Never again'. Don't linger too long or arrive too early, accept generous hospitality without a word of thanks, stay for days and never once offer to help, or arrive with unexpected kids, pets and friends in tow. Treat your hosts with consideration and gratitude, concentrate on giving something in return – your wit, warmth or relaxed company – and you'll be asked back again and again.

Visits and parties

When to arrive Opinions on how late is too late vary in different parts of the country. In most major cities if you are invited for 8pm, no one will arrive before ten past, and you can generally turn up at twenty past or later, and find people just starting on their first drink. Try this in the country and you're liable to make your entrance as your fellow guests finish the soup. Obviously if you're in 'foreign' territory it's safer to plan your arrival fairly close to the stated time. Don't be so zealous though that you get there *early*. Better to drive round the block a couple of times than ring the bell even five minutes before the kick-off, when you could catch your hosts in a state of undress, toys or newspapers all over the sitting room floor and a general air of last-minute panic.

The need for punctuality also varies with the size of the

occasion, and a disgracefully late guest who sneaks into a large throng up to an hour late may well get away with it almost unnoticed, whereas a dinner party can be thoroughly disrupted by one late arrival.

Taking children, pets, other guests Perhaps you'd love to accept an invitation, but it would make life easier to bring along your baby, a dog who can't bear to be parted from you, or a friend who just happens to be staying on that date. Whatever you do, don't spring any of these unexpected extras on your host. Ask him or her first, and ask in such a way that your request can be refused without anyone feeling embarrassed or awkward. If the answer is yes, do your utmost to ensure that babies and pets neither steal the scene with their charm (or at least, not for longer than the first few minutes, after which they should be encouraged to go to sleep quietly), nor cause annoyance with any of their less endearing habits.

Special diets It is only fair to give some warning if you have special dietary needs, such as being vegetarian or having an allergy to certain foods. Mention these when you accept the invitation rather than waiting until the food is in front of you before you start explaining why you can't eat it. Slimming diets are an exception – you can't really expect to be served a calorie-counted meal, especially if you are invited to a lavish spread – so it's better to keep quiet, take small portions and do some discreet removal of cream or butter if you can.

Taking a gift What to take depends on the occasion. It's fine to take a bottle of wine to a dinner party with close friends, but bear in mind that the wine to be served with dinner will already have been chosen and probably opened, so don't necessarily expect to sample your carefully selected bottle during the evening. Be wary of taking wine to people you don't know well. A bottle of supermarket plonk will not be warmly received by someone who drinks nothing but the finest claret. Flowers or special chocolates are a safer bet. If the occasion is a birthday or housewarming take a small appropriate present.

When to leave   Go earlier rather than later, but not too early unless you have made excuses (babysitters, early start next morning) beforehand. The departure of other guests should be a signal, and even if you don't go at the same time it's a mistake to linger on for too much longer. 'Always leave them wanting more' is a good maxim here, so don't wait until your hosts are stifling yawns and looking at their watches.

Saying thank you   Telephone or letter, the choice is yours, but do say thank you and say it promptly, within a couple of days at the most. Phoning is quick but can be slightly awkward unless you also want to chat. A letter or card is often easier (*see* THANK-YOU LETTERS, pages 40–41).

Returning the invitation   When you've been invited to a meal or party it is usual to ask your hosts back within a reasonable time. How long an interval you leave is up to you, but try not to go over six months. Sometimes the thought of entertaining people with whom you have little in common will fill you with horror, but nonethless it should be done. Of course, if you don't want the connection to continue, your failure to return the invitation may do the trick. But when you are likely to see the other people regularly elsewhere, or there is any chance of awkwardness if you fail to invite them, it's better to bow gracefully to the inevitable and take an optimistic view. After all, the return match may be better than you fear.

Dropping in   While some people love receiving unexpected visits, others find them an irritating intrusion, or greet a knock at the door after dark with alarm or suspicion. Phone first if you can and give friends the opportunity to say no. People who aren't expecting callers might be working, sleeping, having a bath, row or hangover and not feel at all like socializing. Realise that if you do drop in unannounced you take a risk. Your arrival might come as a delightful surprise or be the last straw, and people will react accordingly. Be prepared to exit gracefully if it's obvious that you've picked the wrong moment.

Q *I never know what to talk about when I visit friends in hospital. Is it all right to ask about the details of their operation or illness, or should I just behave as if we were meeting in more ordinary circumstances ?*

A Whether friends want to talk about the intricacies of their ailment when in hospital is entirely up to them. You should offer tentative enquiries and let them indicate whether the subject is welcome or not. Certainly this is one occasion when it is acceptable to discuss health and operations, but you shouldn't succumb to any temptation to start talking about your own health. Let the patient have the glory and if necessary listen to as many lurid details as they want to share with you. Otherwise, keep the conversation cheerful, with no messages of gloom, and the visit short. Twenty minutes is long enough, and you should leave sooner if the patient shows signs of tiring. Take a small present such as some light reading matter, fruit or flowers. Try to find out beforehand if the patient feels up to having visitors and respect his or her wishes.

Q *A never-ending stream of callers arrive at my front door, selling anything from cleaning equipment to insurance, collecting money for charities or hawking religious publications. I hate being rude, but frankly I'm seldom interested. What should I do to get rid of them?*

A Unfortunately normal courteous behaviour isn't always sufficient to shift persistent unwanted callers from the doorstep. Strong assertiveness is the only solution. Saying at once: 'Thank you, but I am not interested' as you close the door may feel uncomfortable, but is effective without being downright rude. Charity collecters can be removed politely by donating a small amount to their charity.

Q *The other evening I had put on an old dressing gown and made myself comfortable in front of the TV when there was a knock at the door. Some friends who I don't see often had been passing on their way somewhere else and had decided to drop in on the off chance. I had no option but to ask them in and they stayed for over an hour, so I missed my programme. What should I have done?*

A You would have been quite within your rights to have said that although you were delighted to see them you couldn't ask them in because you were just about to settle down to watch a programme you'd been looking forward to. Then you could have fixed another time and date for them to call round. In reality though that would be difficult to carry off without making everyone feel awkward, and most people would feel obliged to ask their friends in. You could have made it clear that you were pleased to see them but at the same time indicated that they were disturbing you by saying: 'It's lovely to see you – do come in and have a drink. I'm afraid it'll have to be quick though – the last episode of a series I've been watching is on in half an hour and I just can't miss it.'

Staying overnight

When you are invited for a weekend, your hosts should make it clear when you are expected to arrive and leave and, once there, should also tell you about mealtimes and household routines (*see* OVERNIGHT GUESTS, page 82). Make sure you get up in time for breakfast if necessary and pack a good book so that you can take yourself off to bed when the rest of the family retires, even if it is earlier than your usual time.

Try to fit in with the rest of the household as much as

possible. Go along willingly with any activities that have been planned especially for you. Offer help as appropriate with housework or preparations for a meal. Also, leave your room tidy and make your bed in the mornings. Rinse out the bath and basin after use.

Find out whether you will need any special clothes such as boots or waterproofs for country walking, or whether you are expected to dress up for dinner. If you're not sure what the plans are, it's better to ring and ask than to arrive laden with suitcase-loads of clothes to cope with any contingency.

It's a nice gesture to take a gift when you go to stay. Contributions of food and drink are usually very welcome with close friends. For people you know less well consider a plant, flowers or fruit, or some small, unusual item of food (perhaps your own local speciality). If you prefer, send a gift after your visit, when you'll be better able to choose something that your hosts would like.

Always say thank you as you leave (even if you've had a dreadful time). And phone or, better, send a follow-up letter of thanks within a few days as well (*see* THANK-YOU LETTERS, page 40).

Q *Some friends asked us recently if their 18-year-old daughter and a friend could use our weekend cottage for a couple of nights during the week. We don't know their daughter very well and are not happy about saying yes. How can we refuse without being rude?*

A You could say 'Sorry, but we prefer it if only very close friends use the house when we are not there.' Alternatively you could say that although you are sure their daughter would be very careful in the house you always like to have it available mid-week in case you or your own friends can get away.

Q *I spent a weekend from Friday night to Sunday for the first time with friends recently. I made my own bed on Saturday* *morning, but I wasn't sure what to do on the Sunday. Should I have made the bed; stripped it off completely to save my hostess the work, or turned it back and left it for her to strip off the sheets?*

A Either ask if you should strip the bed, or simply turn back the sheets or duvet neatly to the foot of the bed, but leave the bottom sheet in place. That way you show willing by saving your hostess the bother of unmaking a carefully made bed, and also avoid the risk of exposing an aged, spare-bed mattress.

Q *We have been invited to a weekend houseparty by my husband's boss. We know that they have a large country house and employ a full staff, so please could you tell us what to expect, as neither of us have had to deal with maids, butlers and so on before.*

A Your luggage will be taken to your room for you. Your host will serve you with drinks, or invite you to help yourself. You will be told what the plans are for your stay – who the other guests are, whether you are eating in or out and so on. When you leave you should tip members of staff who have helped you: the butler, maid, cook. Give tips in person as far as possible, although you can leave the maid's tip in the bedroom. Ask your host for guidance on how much to leave.

Q *Some friends who have a house in the country are always saying 'You must come and visit us', but they never specify a date. Do you think I could ring them and suggest some possible times, as we would very much like to take up their offer?*

A It would be more tactful to wait until the next time they suggest a visit before you try and fix a date. It's possible that they are just using the 'we must have lunch' ploy, which is not to be taken at face value, rather than issuing a genuine invitation.

Q *I went to a dinner party recently where a few guests helped to take the plates out into the kitchen. To our amazement, our host promptly handed us tea towels, filled the sink and proceeded to wash the lot, obviously expecting us to dry the crockery and put it away. Meanwhile we were missing out on the merriment in the dining room. What should we have done?*

A It was a tricky situation because really the washing up should not have been tackled before the guests had left, so if you had excused yourself it would have been an implied criticism. Once trapped in the kitchen, tea towel in hand, there's not a lot you can do about it except dry up quickly and escape back to the party feeling virtuous.

Q *I took a bottle of wine as a gift for friends who had invited me for the weekend. When we drank it I thought it tasted slightly sour. However, no one else commented, so I kept quiet. Should I have spoken up?*

A Certainly. You should have apologized and made sure that no more of the wine was drunk. Then you could have retrieved the bottle and returned it to the shop for a replacement to give to your friends as soon as possible.

Being a guest at work Whenever you are entertained in the course of your own work, or as a guest of your partner, the impression you make is important. The golden rule is to keep in control. It's never a wise idea to let your hair down good and proper on a work-related occasion, unless you want to be the talk of the office the following day.

It's pretty obvious that a business lunch has a purpose, be it to exchange or extract information, do a deal, or size up the opposition. Remember that you are there to work, not just to have a jolly time, and behave accordingly. Don't get drunk, keep your private life and problems to yourself, and don't be drawn into gossip about others.

The same rules apply when you accompany your partner to an office 'function'. Your role here is to be supportive and discreet. Forget any work secrets to which you are privy, and those juicy nuggets of office gossip. Don't tell the boss that your partner is overworked or unappreciated; or be icy to a colleague whom you know gives your partner a hard time. Be pleasant and friendly to everyone and keep the conversation general (*see also* OFFICE ETIQUETTE, page 23).

Q *At a recent office dance the senior members of staff sat together and danced only with each others' husbands and wives. Was this correct?*

A Ideally senior and junior staff and their partners should mingle at office gatherings and there should be no 'us and them' divisions. However, it is up to senior staff to make sure that this happens, and how much people mix, if at all, will depend on attitudes prevalent within the company.

The dating game

Although in theory these days a woman can ask a man out just as readily as the other way round, in practice a lot of the old rules still seem to apply. Many women still prefer to be asked, and will fight shy of making the first approach. If a man asks a woman out (or vice versa) and she is not interested she should refuse there and then, not say yes and make excuses later. If however she wants to accept but genuinely can't for some reason she should say so, and suggest another day when she is free.

It is up to whoever does the asking to make any arrangements, such as booking tickets or a table, as necessary. The question of who pays has to be negotiated. Some men expect to pay if they ask a woman out, while some women prefer to pay their own way right from the word go. Some couples take it in turn to pay, while others split bills 50/50. These arrangements have to be worked out in the initial stages of the relationship by the two concerned. Even if one person earns much more than the other, it shouldn't be taken for granted that he or she will pay for everything. It is only fair for the other person to offer a contribution or perhaps buy some tickets or cook a meal.

Play it by ear is the only rule, but whoever is footing the bill, the other person should be sensitive enough not to insist on settling up in public if this is likely to cause embarrassment. Better to sort out the finances later, in private, or ensure that agreement is reached over whose turn it is to pay next time.

It's only polite to say thank you at the end of an evening out. And of course, if you want to show interest, you can always ring up a day or two later to say thanks again.

Q *As a single woman I sometimes ask a male friend to accompany me to parties or office functions where I would prefer not to be on my own. However, people who don't know us often assume that he is my boyfriend. How do I make it clear that this is not the case?*

A If you're determined that no-one shall make assumptions, you'll have to introduce your friend saying 'This is my friend John, who's very kindly agreed to come along as my partner this evening.' If that seems a bit blunt you could wait until you get an opportunity to work the information into the conversation. Or if someone very obviously jumps to the wrong conclusion you can put the record straight by saying pleasantly: 'Actually John and I are old friends, and I sometimes persuade him to come along as my partner on this sort of occasion.'

Q *A man at my office is clearly interested in me, and has asked me out several times. I do not want to go out with him and* *always refuse politely, saying I'm too busy. But he never seems to get the message, and always comes back with a suggestion for a different date. How do I persuade him to take no for an answer?*

A People can be extraordinarily thick-skinned if they are determined to succeed. However, in fairness you can't lay all the blame at your admirer's door, because you have gone wrong by implying that you are refusing his invitations because you are too busy to accept, rather than because you don't want to go out with him. You are going to have to be very direct in order to get the message across once and for all. Next time he asks you out, take a deep breath and say: 'I'm sorry if you have got the wrong impression, and I don't want to hurt your feelings, but I don't want to go out with you and that is why I keep refusing your invitations.' Having said that, change the subject or leave the room as soon as you can. Don't get drawn into a discussion of *why* you don't want to go out with him. If he tries to find out, repeat that you simply don't and that's that. Being blunt like this is very hard, but it's far better to be honest than to keep making excuses for the weeks or even months it might take before he gives up.

5

Successful entertaining

To create a successful party, large or small, the hosts have to bring together a number of ingredients. The right blend of people is vital, and of course the food and drink play an important part, as does the general atmosphere which comes from the lighting, music and so on.

To give a party that goes with a real swing is hard work, but very satisfying. Here's how to do it.

Planning

What type of party do you want to have? A five-course dinner for six with all the trimmings? A casual help-yourself supper for a few friends? Early evening drinks for twenty or so? A full-scale celebration with no expense spared? A big, informal, bring-a-bottle party with food and dancing? A Sunday lunch-time buffet in the garden, kids welcome? There are numerous possibilities to choose from depending on how many people you want to invite and how much you want to spend. Whichever type you choose, careful advance organization will make all the difference.

Timing Pick a date for your party at least three weeks ahead to give you time to invite people (*see* INFORMAL INVITATIONS, page 48) and make the arrangements. Lunch parties generally start around 1pm, and the food appears fairly soon after. Dinner is a more moveable feast, usually served between 8 and 9, although it can begin later. Invite people to arrive half an hour or so beforehand for a drink; say '8 for 8.30' on the invitations if you wish.

Early evening drinks or cocktail parties can start at 6–6.30 and you can stipulate a finishing time of around 8.30 or 9 on the invitation, and be fairly sure that all but the stragglers will have left by then. Other evening parties can start between 8 and 9 and go on indefinitely (*but see* GUESTS WHO DON'T LEAVE, page 79).

Whom to ask   Having dealt with the details, you now have to tackle the tricky bit: how many people and whom to ask. Numbers will depend partly on space, but there are other considerations. At a dinner party, six or eight people will easily be able to talk together round the table. More than that and the conversation will break down into smaller groups.

At a 'stand up and shout' party you'll have to decide how many rooms can be used before you calculate numbers. You might want to put food in one room and have dancing in another. Given enough space, you could start off in a smaller room and move to a larger one as more people arrive. Estimate carefully. No one enjoys being crammed in like a sardine, shrieking above the noise in order to be heard, but nor will people relax if the party feels 'empty' because the room is too large. To be on the safe side always invite a few more people to a party than you can comfortably accommodate, as it's very unlikely that everyone you ask will come.

The question of whom to invite is easiest at a large gathering, when the answer is 'anyone and everyone you like.' Big parties are the ideal opportunity to invite people who can be 'difficult' or shy in a smaller group. With a bit of luck, and some judicious introducing from you, they may well find someone else among the throng to chat to happily, and if not they always have the option of moving on.

Planning a balanced guest list is more important at a dinner, where it's crucial that the conversation doesn't grind to a halt half way through the evening, or opposites don't clash embarrassingly. Don't fall into the trap of playing too safe though. One or two catalysts can get the sparks flying and liven up a safely predictable evening no end. There's no need to stick rigidly to even numbers or a 50/50 divide of the sexes. When you invite single friends ask them if they would like to bring someone. If they prefer to come alone don't feel that you have to provide a partner for them, but make sure that you arrange the seating so that they don't feel out on a limb if they are the only single person present.

By all means mix people with different interests and lifestyles, but be a bit sensitive towards their feelings: someone recently divorced, say, might not feel happy as the only single in a sea of married couples; someone unemployed or on a low income might not mix well with wealthier friends. But there are no hard and fast rules. Luck has a lot to do with it, and sometimes the most unlikely combinations work marvellously.

What will you need? Now to the practicalities. It's all very well to decide on a huge party and invite 100 people, but you must be able to cater for them. Make a list of everything you'll need, count up what you own and decide in good time if there's anything you need to buy, borrow or hire.

You'll use lots of glasses for a big party and it's as well to provide more than one per guest, as people tend to lose them as the evening wears on. A local wine merchant should be able to help out with glass hire, which will often be free if you buy your party wine at the same time. Check when you hire whether the glasses can be returned unwashed.

Don't risk using your favourite heirlooms if you're a bit short of plates and cutlery. Depending on the formality of the occasion you can make do with paper plates and plastic cutlery (but make them good quality otherwise they won't stand up to the strain). If you must have the real thing, beg or borrow from friends or hire. Large supplies of paper napkins are essential, especially at barbecues, or if you are serving finger food. And you'll need suitable serving implements for the buffet table.

Also on your list should be ashtrays. Large candles left burning at strategic, safe points around the room help to clear smoke from the air and you can buy special 'smokers' candles' for this purpose. Gather a selection of serving dishes and bowls for a buffet, plus smaller receptacles for crisps, nuts and other nibbles. If you plan to serve coffee later make sure you can muster enough cups, saucers and spoons. For a huge party you might even need the means to make coffee by the gallon.

It's generally easier for people to eat sitting down after serving themselves from a buffet table. Have you enough chairs, and can you improvise to provide some small tables? Don't hide away all the comfy seating. Space permitting, designate a 'quiet' room, where people can sit down and take a break to gather their strength before re-entering the fray.

For all but the smallest of parties you will need help. Enlist family or good friends to hand round food or nibbles and keep glasses replenished. You could even consider hiring help. Students from local colleges may be glad of some pocket money. Put someone in charge of removing empty plates after the meal, loading the dishwasher if you have one, or making a start on the washing up. It's a good idea to wash some items there and then, so that you have a supply of clean plates, glasses and cutlery on hand. You'll need help too to keep ashtrays emptied, coffee poured, main course removed and puddings brought in and so on.

Q *I want to ask a colleague to a dinner party that I am planning and would like him to bring a partner if he wishes. However, although we haven't discussed his private life, I suspect that he is gay. It doesn't bother me at all if he wants to bring a male friend, but how can I tactfully make this clear?*

A Behave as you would with any other colleague and simply ask 'Would you like to bring someone?' It is then up to him to assess how well he knows you, how much of his private life he wants to reveal and who, if anyone, he would like to bring.

Q *My husband and I are planning a coming-of-age party for our 18-year-old son. However, none of us drinks, and we would prefer to have no alcohol at the party. Do I have to mention this when I invite people?*

A There's no obligation to have alcohol at a party, especially one that is being held for a young person. However you could save yourself the embarrassment of people arriving with bottles in hand if you do point out when you invite them that no alcohol will be served.

Q *My girlfriend and I were invited to a party and the invitation said we should 'bring a bottle'. I thought it would be OK to take one bottle from the two of us, but she insisted on taking a second bottle, saying we should give one each. Who was right?*

A The basic idea of bringing a bottle is that each guest provides roughly the amount he or she intends to consume. Most couples would probably take only one bottle from the two of them, but if you feel like being more generous there's certainly nothing to say you shouldn't.

On the day

No matter how well prepared you are, you'll probably do a good deal of last minute organization on the day. And your task doesn't end when the party begins. Hosting is hard work, because it takes effort and attention from start to finish to make a party go well. You simply can't afford to relax too much, because you always have to keep an eye open to see how your guests are faring.

Be on hand to greet people as they arrive, and show them where to leave their coats and tidy up. Tell people when they arrive where the loo is so that they can find it without asking later.

Feeding the masses   Dinner parties are usually small enough for the host to serve fairly easily (*see* SERVING, page 94). At a larger party, it's easier for people to help themselves. You can lay the food out on a table beforehand, and cover it over until feeding time. You'll probably plan to eat an hour or more after the party begins to allow for latecomers to arrive, so do make sure there are some nibbles available earlier on. Most people won't have eaten and will be loathe to start drinking alcohol on an empty stomach.

When you are setting out your magnificent spread, cut the food into portions wherever possible. Not only does this make it easier for people to serve themselves, it also means that less food will be wasted, since when confronted with an appetizing selection of food the temptation is for people to take more than they can actually manage.

Putting guests at ease   If you can get helpers to deal with most of the food, so much the better. As host your task is to oil the wheels of your party. The first priority after guests have disposed of their coats is to get them a drink. You can either do this yourself at a small party, or direct them to a drinks table to help themselves or be served by a helper. Next on the list of priorities is for guests to be introduced. At a small party you can introduce everyone in the room, but above about ten people this becomes too cumbersome and anyway conversation will be in small groups rather than general. Introduce guests to someone they will be able to chat to easily (*see* INTRODUCTIONS, page 50).

Keep an eye on the proceedings throughout the evening. Most guests can look after themselves, but you should watch out for anyone who is looking trapped and rescue them. Watch too for anyone left alone, and introduce them to someone else. And be specially thoughtful over anyone you know to be shy or likely to feel out of things.

If you are mixing colleagues with friends, try to ensure that people from work don't stick together in a corner and talk shop for the entire evening. Introduce them to others early on and try tactfully to keep them from drifting together too much, at least at the beginning of the party.

When people start to leave, help them find their coats. At a large party make sure you are around so that people can find you to say their thanks and good-byes.

Party problems

The great crash Treat spills or breakages calmly. Your reaction will be more convincing if you have taken care to keep valuable possessions, ornaments or tableware out of the way. A guest who spills food or drink should offer to clear up as a matter of politeness, but the host will probably refuse and do a quick cleaning up job as unobtrusively as possible.

Unexpected arrivals You can do nothing but grin and bear it if a guest turns up with an uninvited friend, even if it's someone you loathe. Suppress your wrath for later, and behave with the same consideration as you would show to your invited guests.

The effects of drink What of the guest who gets helplessly drunk? You can go some way to avoiding this by excising from your guest list anyone who is known to get carried away when the wine flows. If you decide to chance inviting a friend with a tendency to overdo it, make sure they come accompanied by someone who is prepared to take them home. Should someone unexpectedly get drunk, try and stop them drinking any more alcohol as soon as you notice what is happening. Remove their glass (and any bottle they may have appropriated). This is a time when you will need a good, sober friend to take the drunken guest home and see him or her safely indoors. If this is not possible, ply the inebriate with quantities of non-alcoholic liquid – water, coffee, fruit juice – anything which will help to counteract the dehydrating effects of alcohol. It takes some time to sober up and your best bet may be to let the guest sleep it off in a spare room until he or she is able to get home. First though, use persuasion to remove car keys and don't return them until you are convinced that he or she is in a fit state to drive.

The majority of drunks eventually fall harmlessly asleep, although they may have done a good deal of giggling and falling around beforehand. The worst types are men or women who become aggressive – either verbally or even physically – when they are feeling the worse for wear. In these unpleasant circumstances get your most persuasive friends to try and calm the situation. Whatever you do, don't allow an argumentative drunk to insist on driving away, no matter how much you'd like to see the back of him or her. Get a friend to offer a lift, or insist that the guest stays and has a lot of coffee and a chance to calm down.

Guests who don't leave   Shifting guests who show no signs of going home when the party is on its last legs requires unsubtle measures. First, offer 'a cup of coffee before you go'. If they're still firmly ensconced ten minutes or so after draining their cups, turn the lights up a bit and start clearing debris into the kitchen. Refuse offers of help politely but firmly, and carry on clearing away. It shouldn't be too long before they take the hint.

Q   *At a party recently, where I knew hardly anyone, I got stuck for nearly an hour with a terribly boring man. He was determined not to let me out of his clutches, and it was ages before my host passed close enough to pick up my frantic signals. How could I have made a tactful getaway?*

A   It's always much easier to escape from a group, where you can drift off unobtrusively with no need for an explanation (you might be going to the loo, after all). Getting trapped with one individual is always tricky, especially if they don't share your desire to move on after a while. Your best bet is to try and lure someone else into the conversation so that the twosome becomes a three-or-more-some and you can then move away without stranding your companion alone. The quest for a fresh drink, even if your companion comes with you, offers a chance to get talking to someone else on route or at the bar. Another possible way to enlarge the group would be to suggest going to talk together to someone else you know at the party.

Seating at dinner parties

At large parties guests can roam from group to group, and may chat to a large number of people during the evening. Smaller dinner parties however, call for the conversation to be sustained for several hours between the same people, and therefore need more careful planning if everyone is to get the most from the occasion.

There was a time when precedent was all, and the hosts had their work cut out establishing who was entitled to sit at the right hand of whom, according to the rigid rules of rank that applied. In those days, the most important female guest (whether by virtue of age or rank) sat on the right of the host, and the hostess was flanked by the two most important male guests.

Now there are no hard and fast rules. Your top priority is to make sure people get a chance to enjoy the company of others, and at a small dinner party it won't much matter who sits where because the conversation can range across the table without any difficulty. Couples, married or otherwise, are generally separated, on the grounds that they have plenty of opportunity to talk to each other the rest of the time. You can alternate men and women around the table if you wish, and if the party consists of even numbers of sexes. Otherwise spread out members of whichever is in the minority fairly evenly. Don't agonize about it too much, but do work out who is to sit where before you all arrive at the table. A very large party might be more easily organized with a seating plan, pinned up where people can look at it before the meal, and individual place cards.

Flexibility is the rule. There is some sense in hosts sitting at opposite ends of the table, with guests between them on either side, simply because in this way they can oversee both ends of the table and make sure that everyone is served, glasses are refilled and so on. However, if the arrangement of the room means that the one host would rather sit elsewhere so as to be near a heated tray, or the kitchen, or to have enough elbow room for serving, then so be it. No one is going to worry.

With a larger number of guests, seat people near those with whom they are likely to have most in common, so that if the conversation breaks down into smaller groups they will be well placed. People will have a better chance to talk to everyone if you suggest that they move around when the coffee is served. Use your judgement on this, and don't disrupt things if people are already happily chatting. If you do sense a lull, a change can make all the difference and revive a party that is temporarily flagging. Alternatively, a move to another room for coffee will make a natural opportunity for people to talk to others. And very occasionally the old custom is still observed by which women leave the room while the men drink port.

Q *My elderly aunt, who is quite a character, is coming to stay and I am planning to invite a few people to dinner one evening while she is with us. She loves meeting people and talking, but the problem is that she is rather deaf and won't easily be able to join in general conversation. Should I seat her between myself and my husband, so that we can make sure she doesn't feel left out?*

A Your aunt will get more out of the evening if, instead of being over-protective, you take a few precautions to make sure that she is treated considerately. Keep the gathering small, as the greater the volume of general noise, the harder it is for people to make themselves heard. Invite people who you know are patient and tolerant. Warn the other guests that your aunt is hard of hearing, but emphasize her love of conversation and ask them to remember to speak clearly, and to be prepared to repeat anything she has missed. Sit your aunt on your husband's right (where she belongs, strictly speaking, since the party is in her honour) and put an interesting conversationalist on her other side.

Overnight guests

Preliminaries When you invite people to stay for a few days or a weekend, it is helpful to make it clear roughly when you expect them to arrive and leave. You can do this tactfully by offering to meet a train on say, Friday night, and suggesting that 'we drop you back to the station Sunday after tea, in time for the 5 o'clock', or whatever. If they are coming by car you can say something like 'We'll have a cold supper on Friday, so it doesn't matter if you can't get here until 8.30 or 9. And I'll make sure that lunch is in good time on Sunday so that you don't get caught up in the early evening rush'.

It's helpful also to give people an idea of what you have planned for their stay so that they can pack accordingly. This is especially important if they are going to need to dress up, or you are planning wet and muddy walks that call for boots or can offer sports, swimming, riding or other activities.

The guest room Check the guests' rooms before they arrive, especially if children are being evicted to make space, and ensure that there'll be no need to be disturb them once they arrive because some vital item has been left in their quarters. Provide towels and some clothes-hanging space plus coat-hangers and an empty drawer or two. A couple of paperbacks or magazines for insomniacs, a water glass, a few biscuits, some sweets or fruit for late night snacks and a portable radio, if you have a spare, will all be useful. And a few flowers will brighten up the room and make it welcoming.

A subtle itinerary Up to a point you can gently organize your guests when they are staying with you, while not making them feel regimented. Help them feel more at ease when they arrive by telling them about the routines of the household: when the bathroom is likely to be free, hints on the workings of idiosyncratic plumbing, or tricky door locks, how to deal with the attentions of family pets and so on.

Guests will also want to know about mealtimes and should fall in with your wishes. But tell them the truth. It's no good saying 'Have breakfast whenever you like' if you need the table cleared and lunch under way by 10 am. Offering breakfast in bed is a good way of giving guests a lie in and at the same time keeping them out of your way in the rush first thing.

When your guests do emerge, be ready with some idea of how you expect them to spend their time. If the idea is that they amuse themselves during the day, and you meet up again later on, it will be helpful to point them in the direction of interesting shops, places to visit, pleasant walks, tennis courts, the beach or whatever the local attractions are. Keep a few guide books or local maps for visitors. Also, give them an idea of when you expect them back. Should the weather mean that outdoor pursuits are off, tell them which room they can use to relax in comfort and offer books, magazines or papers, music or TV.

Don't refuse if guests offer help. Most people like to feel they are contributing something, and won't feel at all at ease if their hosts are tearing around in a frenzy, while they sit idly with their feet up.

Sleeping arrangements Generally these are not a problem. Unmarried couples who are in a well-established relationship or who live together can be put in a double bed and the only exception would be to spare the feelings of an aged relative who might be shocked by this arrangement. In that case, explain the problem to the couple in advance and apologize.

However, if you don't know what stage a couple's relationship has reached, you have two choices. Either put them in separate rooms and ignore any sounds of late night visiting, or ask the woman beforehand if she would prefer to share a room.

Q *My 19-year-old daughter is away from home at university. She wants to bring her boyfriend, who we haven't met, home to stay during the Christmas holidays. Should I put them in the same room? Our family has always been rather reticent about these matters, and to tell the truth I'm embarrassed about asking her.*

A The best solution would certainly be to try and over-come your hesitation and ask her straight out. But if this really is not possible, then it is potentially less embarrassing all round to assume that they will want separate rooms, rather than put them together.

Q *My 20-year-old daughter, who has always been very open with us, has told us that she is a lesbian and that she is sharing a flat with her partner, who is another woman. They want to come and stay with us for a few days, but although we have tried hard to accept her lifestyle I still balk at the idea of putting them in a double bed. I don't want to risk upsetting my daughter or her friend. How do I cope with this situation please?*

A It sounds as though you have a good relationship with your daughter, which might enable you to talk this problem over and explain your feelings. When she stays in your house she should certainly comply with your wishes, regardless of how she lives her life at other times. A compromise to consider might be to put her and her partner in the same room with separate beds. This might make you feel easier and would not cause any comment among visitors or other family members, in a situation that, unfortunately for your daughter and her friend, is still found unacceptable in many circles.

Children's parties

Most parents find themselves faced with organizing a birth-day party for children at some time or another. A child's party can be as simple or as lavish as you can afford, but it needs to run like clockwork in order not to turn into chaos.

Invitations should be written and sent out in advance, so

that the children's parents know date, starting and finishing time, address and occasion. Let your child invite his or her friends, who should all be roughly the same age. Children who have previously invited your child to parties should also be included, regardless of whether they are counted as friends.

Guests at a birthday party should bring a small present. And all guests should be given a gift to take home with them. Parents should drop their children off on time and then leave, as the last thing the host parents want is loitering adults who need to be entertained. However some adult help will be needed, even for a small party.

Work out a list of boisterous games to start off with, followed by an earlyish tea and quieter games afterwards. Save professional entertainment if you are having it, to the end.

Parents should of course return promptly at the time stated to collect their exhausted offspring.

Q *Do I need to send a thank-you note to the parents of my 7-year-old son's friend when he has been to a birthday party at their home?*

A No, there's no need to be so formal, you can simply say thanks (and make sure your son does too) when you collect him.

Entertaining on business

Normal courtesy between men and women should apply at work as elsewhere, although it may be modified for the sake of convenience, especially if women are in the minority. It could cause problems if say, 12 men had to ensure that two women preceeded them through every door en route from meeting room to restaurant. It is more likely that others would stand back to allow the most senior person present, man or woman, to precede them. Some men in business still find it hard to deal with a woman of equal or greater seniority, and women need to make allowances for this.

Although more and more women are taking on jobs where they are expected to entertain male clients, this can still seem a slightly unnerving prospect, particularly for a woman who is relatively new to this role.

In this situation, her first priority should be to get herself known at one or two nearby restaurants. Once she has done this she can relax, knowing that the staff will treat her as being 'in charge' of lunch and will automatically take the order from her and give her the bill.

As hostess it is the woman's job to choose and taste the wine, but she can of course ask the approval of her guest, having made her choice. As an alternative to eating in a restaurant, and for a 'working' lunch, where business has to be discussed, as opposed to a more sociable occasion, it's worth considering laying on a buffet meal in the office if this is possible.

All the rules about making the right impression (*see* BEING A GUEST AT WORK, page 68) apply just as much if you are hosting the lunch as if you are the guest. Be careful not to drink too much or to be indiscreet. Stick to business and steer clear of gossip or personal details. Having a good idea before lunch of what you hope to achieve helps keep the conversation focussed in the right direction.

Entertaining foreign clients   Much of the time, when dealing with business contacts from Europe or America, the 'rules' of etiquette are much the same as in Britain. However, some other cultures do have different customs which should be understood and observed.

Muslims, for instance, cannot eat pork or drink alcohol. During Ramadan, which lasts for a month and falls at a slightly different time each year, a Muslim fasts completely between dawn and dusk, taking no food or drink and not smoking. Women are likely to have problems dealing with Arab clients, who come from countries where the status and role of women is so different from that of the UK. When mixing socially with people of this religion women should dress modestly to avoid causing offence.

Japanese business people have customs which are noticeably different from British ones. They are very courteous, bow to each other instead of shaking hands (although Westerners are not expected to bow when meeting Japanese) and do not generally discuss business at the first meeting. Business cards are exchanged as a matter of course with every new contact. It is not usual to call a Japanese by his or her first name. Instead you should add the suffix 'san' to the surname, so that Mitsubishi-san means Mrs, Miss or Mr Mitsubishi. The Japanese consider it impolite to answer a question with No; and a Yes does not necessarily mean that your guest agrees with you – it can merely mean that he has understood what you have said.

Q *When I take clients out to lunch should I choose the restaurant, or am I supposed to ask them where they would like to go?*

A It's up to you to choose the restaurant, but if you like you can ask your guests which type of food they would prefer.

Q *I have to entertain three male clients to lunch to discuss an important deal. Although I know I'll be fine once the 'meeting' gets going, I'm always a little nervous at first. Have you any suggestions?*

A Don't have a stiff aperitif to calm your nerves (or if you do, have one only and keep it small). Go easy on alcohol during the meal. Sip your wine, and have a glass of water alongside it. Choose a restaurant where you know the service is unobtrusive and good, so that you won't be distracted. Arrange to meet your guests at the restaurant and schedule your own arrival ten minutes or so early. This will give you a chance to comb your hair, get settled at the table and have a quick look at the menu to choose your own meal so that when your guests arrive you can give them your full attention straight away.

Q *I took a man who heads our sister organization to lunch to discuss business, but although I had quite clearly invited him, to my fury he took charge of the proceedings. He ordered the food, grabbed the wine list and chose the wine and I had a job to stop him paying. How should I have dealt with him?*

A No matter how livid you were you should have concealed your feelings and given in gracefully. Once you'd got the measure of your guest, a sensible strategy would have been to have left the table for a few moments to visit the ladies room and taken the opportunity to pay the bill or at least handed over a credit card and asked for the payslip to be prepared and presented to you for signature.

6

Eating and drinking

For most people, everyday entertaining is a fairly casual business, where no one is going to worry over-much if the side knives have been forgotten, or the soup spoon is in the wrong place. Even so, it's always pleasing to create a relaxed mood where the meal runs smoothly and there are no mishaps to create a disturbance. And at other times special guests make it important to get every detail just right, or an invitation arrives to a dinner party that promises to be more formal than usual. Whatever the nature of the occasion it's useful to have a working knowledge of what goes where on the table, and feel at home with the mechanics of coping gracefully with awkward foods.

Setting the table

The table can be spread with a cloth or left uncovered to show off its surface. A table mat is put at each place and these should be large enough to prevent spills damaging the table if there is no cloth.

Also on the table go serving spoons; mats for vegetable dishes; candles (positioned with an eye to safety, not too near the edge or within range of gesticulating guests); salt, pepper and mustard if needed (more than one set if possible for a large number); butter and knife; ashtrays if you are happy for people to smoke at the table. Flowers or table decorations can be added for colour, but keep them fairly low or very high so that they don't dazzle or block the cross-table view.

Customs concerning the arrangement of cutlery, glasses and plates on a table do serve a purpose, because they mean that every diner can unerringly select the right implement for each course and will not find him or herself faced with food and no appropriate cutlery.

Cutlery Forks go on the left, prongs upwards; knives (with blades facing inwards) and spoons on the right. The basic rule is to use the cutlery starting at the outside and working in. However, identify the butter knife first, as it may be placed on the extreme right of the setting (otherwise it will be laid across the top of the setting or on the side plate). Spoon and fork for pudding can be placed on either side of the setting or, less formally, across the top.

If fish is served, fish knives and forks can be used. However, they are generally regarded as something of an anachronism, and are by no means essential.

Plates The side plate is used for bread and is placed on the left of the setting. Bread served as an accompaniment to the meal should be broken into small pieces as you want it, and each piece buttered individually before eating. This custom saves you tackling the impossible task of taking an elegant, crumbless bite out of a large piece of crusty bread. Help yourself to butter using the butter knife (not your side knife) and put it on the edge of your plate. The side plate can also be used for cheese, and is moved to the centre of the setting when the cheese is served.

Salad can be served on the side plate, in which case clean side plates should be provided for cheese. Alternatively, the salad can be eaten from a smaller plate placed at the top centre, above the dinner plate, where it is easily reached, but doesn't interfere with side plate or glasses.

A finger bowl may be provided with food that is to be eaten with the fingers. Dabble your fingers in the water and dab them dry on your napkin. Occasionally in restaurants hot towels may be provided for diners to wipe their fingers with. These generally come sealed in wrappers, which should be opened, the towel used and replaced in the basket or dish in which it was brought to the table.

Glasses The wine glass is placed on the right of each place setting, above the knife. If more than one wine is being served there should be a different glass for each type.

Different shapes of glass can be used for red and white wines although this is not essential and a standard goblet can be used for both.

Many people like to drink water with their meal as well as wine, so a water glass should be provided at each setting next to the wine glass, and a jug of iced water placed on the table for people to help themselves.

Liqueur, port or brandy glasses can be grouped with the other glasses from the start of the meal, but the table will be less cluttered if these are provided separately for those who want them at the end of the meal.

Napkins   Plain white linen napkins always look good, but napkins can be made of other fabric in a colour or pattern to complement the table setting. For less formal occasions paper napkins can be used, but make them good quality, thick ones of a generous size. Bear in mind that coloured paper napkins can stain clothes if food or drink is spilled on them.

Napkins can be folded into shapes ranging from a water lily to a bishop's mitre in which case they should stand proudly in the centre of each place setting. A simpler approach is to fold them into a triangle, oblong or square and place them on the side plate.

Guests should unfold the napkin and place it on the lap (or tuck it in under the chin if eating spaghetti bolognaise and wearing white). It is used for wiping the fingers or mouth and at the end of the meal is left scrunched up on the table, not refolded.

Q *I have never possessed a dinner service, but instead have accumulated a collection of odd bits and pieces of china of different shapes and sizes. The only thing they have in common is that all are decorated in blue and white. Now I have taken a new job which requires me to do some fairly formal entertaining at home. Must I ditch my charming miscellany in the interests of doing the right thing?*

A No, but you may need to supplement it. There is no

rule that says all china must match, and a mixture of styles can produce a very appealing effect. However, what you must beware of is if the plates vary so widely in size that some of your guests are eating their main course from a plate half the size of their neighbour's. Add to your selection until you are satisfied that you can provide your maximum number of guests with plates and bowls of roughly similar dimensions for soup, starter or salad, bread, main course and pudding.

All about food

Whenever you are planning a meal for guests, give careful consideration to the food. The only rule, and one which you should not ignore, is know your own limitations. Choose dishes you are sure you can produce successfully and don't be tempted to experiment except among close friends who will respond kindly to a disaster. Now is not the time to switch ambitiously into *cordon bleu* mode if your usual style of cooking is fuss-free and straightforward.

Another factor is how much time can you afford to spend on preparation. If you're a demon cook, for whom no detail is too much trouble, then all well and good. But that's not to say you can't produce an excellent meal if you pack all the preparation into the night before. Attractive presentation and a balanced menu are guaranteed to please your guests, and it matters not a jot if you prepare the food simply, as long as you do it well.

Planning the courses For any meal but the most informal supper the minimum number of courses you can get away with is three: starter or soup, main and pudding. You can pad this out to mammoth proportions by adding fish and/or a sorbet between starter and main course; including cheese, fruit and salad as separate courses (see opposite for where to slot them in) and finishing off with a savoury after the pudding. However this would create a meal of Edwardian banquet proportions, so bear in mind today's more meagre appetites and tailor the menu to leave guests feeling pleasantly satisfied rather than stuffed to the gills.

Aim for balance and contrast. Avoid too many rich or creamy dishes at one meal. There's no need for everything to be breathtakingly spectacular. One dish on which you've really gone to town will have far more impact than half a dozen jostling for the limelight. And remember, a bowl of perfect young vegetables adorned only by a knob of butter, can be just as appetising as a far more elaborate dish. Follow a light course with something heavier, a spicy dish with one that's blander and refreshing. And weigh the tastes and textures against each other, being careful not to choose the same predominant ingredient or flavour for more than one dish.

Buffet parties are a good way of entertaining a lot of people at the same time, but it is up to the hosts to make sure that the food can be eaten easily, especially if there is a shortage of seating. Don't serve jacket potatoes, chicken joints, green salad or anything that needs a knife and fork if you are expecting people to consume their meal standing up. Instead choose forkable items, and cut things up into bite-sized pieces.

What to serve when Which comes first, the cheese or the pudding? Many people prefer to follow the French style, and serve the cheese immediately after the main course. In that case, it makes sense to carry on drinking the same red wine that accompanied the main course. But there are those who swear by a tangy piece of cheese (and perhaps a glass of port) as the ideal way to round off a meal and clear the sweetness of the pudding from the palate. Neither is wrong, so you can decide for yourself, or ask your guests which they would prefer.

At a simple, pud-less meal, cheese and fresh fruit can be brought to the table together after the main course, and guests can pick and choose at will.

Salad is the other puzzler. You can treat it as a course in its own right, in which case bring it on after the main course has been eaten. Or it can make its appearance with the main dish, and people can decide for themselves whether to eat it with their meat or save it to the end. The choice is open.

Serving suggestions Serving always presents a problem at a dinner party. Try and do it with the minimum of interruption to the conversation, but interject a tactful reminder if necessary to get people to serve themselves if they are so deep in talk that others are being kept waiting.

The most informal approach is to put all the dishes into the middle of the table and let your guests have a free-for-all. Easier perhaps is to let guests help themselves to vegetables and serve the main dish for them. You can do this in the privacy of the kitchen, or from your place at the table. Women can be served before men, or you can follow tradition and serve the woman seated to the host's right first and then proceed clockwise round the table. At a very formal dinner, all dishes are served to the guests in which case the food is served from the left and the plates removed from the right. (*See* SERVING YOURSELF, page 99; ALL ABOUT DRINK, page 102.)

Carving This is something of an art form, and best practised privately before staging a public performance. You can of course produce the tantalizingly roasted joint for approval, and then whisk it away to be carved in the kitchen. You will need a proper carving knife, well-sharpened; a carving fork with safety catch and a steady hand.

Q *I gave a dinner party at rather short notice last week and as there was so little time to prepare I spent a fortune and bought the food ready-prepared from the local supermarket. It was all delicious, and my guests were bowled over and full of praise for the meal. I was rather embarrassed, but thanked them for their compliments without letting on that I hadn't lifted a finger. Should I have come clean?*

A Not at all – you provided your guests with an excellent meal on which they were quite right to compliment you. How you did it is your affair.

How to tackle tricky food

It's well worth learning the techniques required to dispatch difficult foods neatly, if only because some of the items on this list are special treats which should definitely not be missed without good reason (*see* CUTLERY KNOW-HOW, page 99).

Artichokes Take off the leaves one at a time with your fingers, and dip the fleshy base into the sauce or butter provided. Use your teeth to strip off the delectable morsel and discard the rest of the leaf on the edge of the plate. The leaves near the heart have no flesh and are simply removed until the 'furry' choke is exposed. This should be uncovered by scraping away the 'thistle' at the base and the flesh eaten with knife and fork.

Asparagus Pick up the spear in your fingers, and dunk the tip into the melted butter or sauce served with your portion. Bite off the end – you can do this in a couple of goes, dipping again in between – and place the last couple of inches, which are too fibrous to eat, on the edge of the plate.

Caviar If served with toast fingers, use a knife to coax the caviar on to the toast. May also be served on its own in a small pot, in which case eat with a small spoon.

Cheese Don't cut the tip off a V-shaped piece of cheese. Instead, cut yourself a thin slice from one of the longest edges. Different knives may be provided for each cheese to avoid transferring the flavours. You'll get most enjoyment from cheese if you eat your selection in ascending order of strength.

Corn on the cob Can't be done without making a mess, so position your napkin accordingly. Pick up the buttery cob by both ends (little 'handles' may have been driven into the corn to make this easier) and gnaw.

Crab   A dressed crab will have been replaced in its shell and is easily eaten with knife and fork. A whole crab should come with a variety of implements, which you use to crack the claws and pick out the flesh, and to scrape the meat out of the shell. Time-consuming, but worth it.

Fish   If you have been provided with a plate for bones the best option is to fillet a whole fish before you start eating. Do this by running the tip of your knife down the backbone. Slide the flat knife blade into the fish and gently lift the flesh off the bones, leaving the skeleton whole. Remove the other side in the same way. Failing this, you will have to fillet the fish a mouthful at a time, gradually building up a heap of bones at the side of the plate. Remove stray bones from your mouth discreetly and place them with the others. In a restaurant, the waiter will usually offer to fillet a whole fish for you.

Fresh fruit   At a formal meal use the cutlery provided to cut up and peel (if you wish) large fruit like apples and pears. If you have been given a fruit fork, use it to eat the pieces, otherwise eat them with your fingers. For grapes, use the scissors provided to cut a small clump for your plate. Don't spit the pips, but remove them from your mouth into your fingers and place on the side of your plate. Do the same with cherry stones.

Game   If you are served with a whole bird, such as grouse or quail, split the bird in two down the breastbone, then cut the flesh off with your knife and fork. Pick up the bones in your fingers to get at the last of the meat (wait for someone else to do so first, if in doubt).

Lobster   Another messy but very rewarding shellfish. Use your fingers and the 'nutcrackers' and forked pick provided to extract the flesh from the shell.

Mussels Pick the half shells up with your fingers and take out the mussel with a fork. Place the empty shells on a separate plate or around the edge of your dish. Any liquid or sauce can be spooned up like soup after the mussels have been eaten, or drunk from a half-mussel shell, in the French style.

Oysters Swallowed raw. Squeeze lemon over, then hold the shell firmly on the plate with one hand, and use a fork in the other to pick out the oyster. You can then drink the juice out of the shell.

Pâté Spread generously on toast and eat with fingers.

Peas Spear a couple with the fork prongs, then balance a few more on top. Failing that, press them into mashed potato or other sticky substance on the back of the fork. Or flout convention, and go for the American style, turning the fork over and taking it in your right hand to scoop the peas up. This technique is best saved for less formal occasions.

Peking duck Take one of the thin pancakes from its steamer, spread it with a little plum sauce and place on it some fragments of crispy duck and a few bits of chopped cucumber and spring onion. Roll up neatly and eat with the fingers. Don't be too greedy otherwise the filling will spurt out when you take a bite.

Prawns Large whole ones must be shelled. Pull off the head, then open out the undersides of the body shell so that they unpeel. Finally remove the tail. Eat with fingers.

Salad Leafy salads, dripping with dressing, are almost impossible to manage with fork alone, so use a knife as well.

Snails Pick each snail up with the tongs and use the pick to winkle out the flesh. Dip into melted butter before eating and use bread to mop up any remaining butter at the end.

Soup The polite way to eat soup is by pushing the spoon across the bowl away from you, so that any drips fall into the plate, and drinking the soup, quietly, from the side of the spoon. Tip the bowl away from you to get the last few drops.

Spaghetti Hard to eat neatly, without a modicum of sucking and splattering of sauce. Not likely to be served at a formal dinner. Use a fork, plus a spoon if you need one. Spear the fork into the midst of the spaghetti, then lift it out, twirling gently to encourage the pasta strands to wind themselves into a plausible mouthful.

Whitebait Eat them whole, heads and all.

Table manners

Why, in this informal age, are the old rules not waived completely? Because so many of them are founded on common sense. For instance, a person who plants an elbow on the table will, of necessity, lean forward as he or she does so, and thus block the neighbours' view.

It's never pleasant to witness someone talking with mouth open, slurping, chomping, finger-licking or bone-gnawing. Of course among friends and family you can relax more. But at a dinner party it's considerate to behave with a little more restraint. Pace your consumption. Don't gobble, but equally don't slow down so much that your plate is only half emptied when everyone else is ready for the next course. If you are host, encourage guests to start eating as soon as they have been served, while the food is still hot. However, guests should start only if everyone else is showing signs of doing so.

Other things that may pass muster *en famille*, but should be avoided outside your own four walls include taking a second helping before being offered one and picking your teeth (best done behind a closed bathroom door, no matter how tantalizing a morsel is trapped). You can use a piece of bread to mop up the last delicious drops of sauce at an informal dinner and the cook will probably be thrilled by your obvious appreciation. But don't do it at a formal dinner. Unlike the French, the British are still rather inhibited when it comes to obvious enjoyment of their food.

Smokers should ask the host and other guests before lighting up at the table, and should be prepared to take no for an answer. No one should smoke until the end of the meal, and at formal dinners it is incorrect to light up until after the loyal toast.

Remember that as a guest you are expected to 'earn' your dinner by talking to the other guests and generally being good company. By all means offer to help your host, but don't insist if your offer is refused. It disrupts the evening to have too many people milling around during the meal. If it's your party, get organized so that the minimum of trekking backwards-and-forwards is needed.

Guests should talk to both neighbours during the evening. No one person should hog the conversation, and nor should anyone sit in silence (*see* MAKING CONVERSATION, page 54).

Serving yourself   At a formal dinner, you may be offered a dish by a waiter from your left. Pick up the serving implements, take as much as you want and replace them side by side in the serving dish. You can refuse wine if you wish. Cover your glass momentarily with your hand, or just say 'No thank you'. Ask for water if you want it.

Serving at informal dinners may be most easily accomplished by the guests serving themselves or each other from dishes which they pass round the table. If another guest offers to hold a dish for you, or to serve you, accept only if this looks feasible. Don't be afraid to say that it would be easier if you served yourself, or to help hold a heavy dish, or suggest that the dish is put down on the table. Any of these is preferable to ending up with your portion served into your lap.

It is not polite to refuse a course, unless you can't eat the food for some reason such as a health or diet problem. On some occasions you may feel more comfortable to accept a tiny portion, toy with it, and leave it uneaten, than sit with an empty plate.

Cutlery know-how The point of using cutlery properly is that it is more efficient that way, and also it means that you won't be in danger of digging your neighbours in the ribs.

To hold a knife correctly put thumb and index finger on top and in control fairly near the blade and use the other fingers to steady the handle. Don't hold it too tightly, or grasp it like a pen with thumb underneath. Always hold the fork with prongs downwards except when tackling peas or rice, when you can usually get away with turning it over and transferring it to your right hand. Of course, some dishes are eaten with fork only at informal suppers and then you can use the fork, prongs upwards, in the right hand to scoop up the food. When you eat a pudding with a spoon and fork, hold the fork prongs down in the left hand, and use it to help the food on to the spoon. If you stop eating momentarily during the meal, lay your knife and fork on opposite sides of the plate, at angles to each other. This indicates to a waiter that you have not finished, and your plate will not be whipped away. When you have finished, place cutlery neatly together on the plate or bowl.

When you are presented with food which comes with its own cutlery – lobster or snails for instance – and don't know how to tackle it, the simple solution is to ask. You will usually find that people fall over themselves to help and offer advice, demonstrations, warnings and so on. Alternatively keep quiet, watch to see how others tackle the food then follow suit (*see* HOW TO TACKLE TRICKY FOOD, page 95).

Chopsticks Hold the top chopstick like a pen, between thumb and forefinger, about two thirds of the way along, nearest the tip. The lower one rests on the joint of the thumb, and is controlled by the middle and fourth finger. Use your thumb and forefinger to move the top chopstick and with practice you should be able to pick up individual grains of rice or larger pieces of food quite easily. Tackle pieces of meat by tearing them apart with the points of the chopsticks. This can be tricky unless the meat is very tender. When you have finished, balance the chopsticks together across the bowl or place them on the porcelain chopstick rest if one is provided. Japanese chopsticks are different in shape and have very thin pointed ends for eating sushi.

Eating at parties   There is no good solution to the age old problem of how to juggle glass, plate and fork at a buffet party. It is possible to buy small plastic 'trays', which combine a plate compartment with a holder for the glass, or 'glass clips' which fit on to standard plates, but either of these can be rather awkward to use. A thoughtful host will have worked out the answer to the problem for you and provided enough tables, places to put glasses and so on.

Social embarrassments   Apologize if you drop or spill something, but try not to create too much fuss. Offer to help clear up or to pay cleaning bills, whatever seems appropriate, but don't go on apologizing for too long. The host should clear up as much as possible (preferably without getting the vacuum cleaner out) and then forget the incident (*see* THE GREAT CRASH, page 78).

If you feel a cough or sneeze coming on, turn your head away and cover your nose and mouth with handkerchief or hand. Should someone start to choke at the table, offer them water if they don't quickly recover. If you are choking badly, leave the table and make for the bathroom. However, someone who swallows a large bone or appears to be asphyxiating needs immediate help from others.

A belch that slips out can be ignored, or covered up by a cough, a laugh, or a quiet 'I beg your pardon' interjected without pausing into the current sentence. Use whichever seems appropriate to the company. Audible wind of other kinds really has to be ignored or laughed off. Either way it's embarrassing. You could try staring accusingly at the dog.

Q *OK, I know I smoke like a chimney. Just tell me, is it ever acceptable to smoke between courses?*

101

A Only if all the other guests do so. Realistically, this is unlikely in today's anti-smoking climate.

Q *Professional waiters and waitresses serve food so dextrously, using fork and spoon in the same hand. Is that how I'm supposed to serve myself when offered food at a formal dinner?*

A There's no need to compete with the pros, and you risk catapulting the food across the table if you get it wrong. Safer by far to use fork in one hand and spoon in the other to lift the food on to your plate.

All about drink

So much is written about wine that it shouldn't be too difficult to find guidance. A good wine merchant will also be glad to help you choose.

What to offer   At a drinks party, offer a choice of a fairly light red wine and a medium-dry white wine. Of course you can also offer spirits if finances allow and have beer or cider for those who prefer them. It's essential to have mineral water, soft drinks and fruit juices for drivers and non-drinkers. And do offer some sort of stomach-lining food, even if it is only light nibbles, to help absorb the alcohol and save your guests from terrible hangovers.

For a dinner party you will want to choose wine to complement the food, but this doesn't mean that you have to stick to the old rules of white with fish, red with meat. Some light red wines can be served cool or chilled and go perfectly well with fish. And many people prefer to stick to one colour – often white – right through the meal. Below are a few guidelines, which are very flexible:

*aperitifs can include gin and whisky with mixers; sherry, which may be served on ice; and white wine
*sherry can also be served with soup
*save really full-bodied red wines for rich game dishes or

well-flavoured red meat dishes. They will seem too heavy for
white meats
*rosé can be very pleasant, especially in the summer, but
choose a dry one
*mineral water or iced plain water should be on offer
throughout the meal for those who want it
*a glass of a sweet white dessert wine or champagne can be
served with pudding
*cheese is best accompanied by red wine or port

Wine tips   To enjoy wine at its best, it should be served at
the right temperature. Reds develop their full flavour at room
temperature, although beaujolais may be chilled. White
wines, champagne and rosé should be chilled but not so cold
that they become tasteless. You can keep them at the right
temperature in an ice bucket or wine cooler if you have one.

Open red wines an hour or more before serving. Old red
wines and vintage port are generally decanted, leaving behind the sediment which gathers at the bottom of the bottle.
You can start serving the wine as soon as the meal begins or
wait until the starter is finished, as you prefer. Fill the glasses
about two-thirds full. If there is more than one type of wine
a different glass should be provided for each and guests
should try to finish one type with its course before moving
on to the next.

Liqueurs, brandy and port   Liqueurs are served in small
glasses and are usually drunk with the coffee. Brandy is
served in special brandy glasses (balloons), designed to
capture the heady aroma of the spirit. It is generally drunk
neat at the end of a meal, although you can ask for soda if
you prefer it diluted. Port is considered a dessert wine and
so can be drunk with cheese or pudding at the end of the
meal. Traditionally port was the province of the gentlemen,
who consumed it while they smoked their cigars after the
ladies had retired from the dinner table, and this still happens
occasionally. It was considered unlucky to pass the port anti-
clockwise.

Coffee and tea Once the meal is finished you can all stay seated round the table, or move to another room (which also gives guests the opportunity to use the loo).

Tiny coffee cups look pretty, but contain only a mouthful or so and need constant replenishing. Larger cups (demitasse) are more practical, but you should still offer at least one refill. Coffee can be served black, or with milk or thin cream. You can also offer decaffeinated coffee, or even tea or herbal tisanes which many people prefer to coffee, particularly late at night.

Eating in restaurants

The observation of basic table manners naturally applies just as much in a restaurant as in a private home, if not more. Other people are present and the party should not become so noisy or raucous that it intrudes on others.

Ordering An *à la carte* menu means that each dish is chosen and priced separately. On a *table d'hôte* menu there is a fixed price for the meal, with possibly a small choice for each course. These menus are generally less expensive.

When the order is taken, one person may do all the ordering, but it is easier if everyone in turn asks for their own choice. The starter and main course are ordered at the same time, and the waiter returns after the main course has been cleared away to take the order for dessert.

Waiters To attract a waiter's attention, catch his eye. A good waiter will be on the look out for any customer who needs him, while a bad waiter will be adept at missing your glance. If you can't attract the waiter's attention, say 'Waiter', or 'Excuse me' as he passes, but don't shout from the other end of the room. If he is out of earshot, raise your hand and beckon.

Wine When the wine arrives, the bottle will be shown to whoever is tasting the wine so that the label can be checked. The waiter opens the bottle at the table and pours a small amount into the glass for tasting. Fragments of cork floating in the wine do not mean that it is 'corked'. It is very unusual for a bottle to be 'corked' (that is, sealed with a faulty cork so that the wine has gone off), and if it is it will smell and taste dreadful. The waiter should then be asked to remove it and provide another bottle.

Once opened and accepted the glasses will be filled and the bottle will be left on the table, if red, or possibly in an ice bucket if white, depending on how smart the restaurant is. The waiter may return periodically to top up the glasses, or this can be done by the diners.

Complaints Sometimes food arrives which is not what was ordered or has not been cooked as requested, or a dish may be cold, or taste strange. When this happens diners must have the courage of their convictions, call the waiter, explain the problem and ask for a replacement. This has to be done confidently, and the waiter should remove the offending dish without argument and replace it as soon as possible.

Q *Four of us were eating in a restaurant the other night, and a couple at a nearby table had their two children with them. About half way through the meal these children clearly got bored, because they started to run around the restaurant, shouting and making a noise. Their parents took no notice of this behaviour, but our meal was ruined. Should we have complained to the parents, or to the waiter?*

A You should have called the waiter, told him that the children's behaviour was ruining your meal, and doubtless other people's too, and asked him to request the parents to keep their children quietly under control at their own table.

7

What to wear

'Wear what you like', must be the most unhelpful advice ever given to a perplexed guest. Although most people dress to please themselves and choose clothes with an eye to personal taste as well as to convention, few of us enjoy feeling conspicuous or out of place because we're dressed differently from everyone else. Selecting the right 'uniform' for the occasion inspires confidence, and helps us feel at ease.

Everyday dress

Whenever you can, ask your hosts what they will be wearing. If doubt strikes as you begin your rummage through the wardrobe, save yourself the anguish of wondering if you've misjudged the situation completely and phone to ask 'Are you dressing up?' If for any reason this is not possible, opt to underdress rather than overdress, on the grounds that it's less embarrassing to appear in an unadorned black frock when all around are in satin and taffeta, than vice versa. Don't overdo the understated look though, as you risk offending your hosts if they get the impression that you thought it wasn't worth making an effort.

Women's clothes Accumulate a few simple evening outfits that make you feel comfortable and good and you'll never be at a loss. Silk shirts, evening trousers, pretty skirts, the ubiquitous black dress and some judicious jewellery can take you to dinner parties, drinks or the theatre and always look right.

As far as working clothes are concerned, everything depends on what you are doing. The right outfit can range from a smart suit to jeans and you can gauge the level of smartness from observing how colleagues dress and using them as a yardstick. Take extra care over your appearance for a job interview. Even if casual clothes are readily acceptable in your particular field, they won't create the right impression if they are grubby or crumpled.

Clothes which have an 'evening' look about them – made in shiny or flimsy fabrics, or cut revealingly – are generally out of place at the office. An expanse of cleavage which is dashing at a party can be disconcerting in an important meeting.

Trousers are acceptable almost everywhere these days, although jeans may be too casual in many work settings and smart restaurants.

The best thing about trousers is the ease of movement which they afford the wearer. Getting in and out a car while wearing a skirt for instance, particularly if it is short and straight, can be a hideously inelegant manoeuvre. The neatest way of getting in is to sit down on the side of the seat first and then swing your legs in, keeping feet and knees together. If the car is very low, steady yourself with a hand on the dashboard. When you get out, put your left foot on the pavement, bring your knees together, put the right foot on the pavement and stand up. This takes practice, but is a skill worth learning.

Men's clothes For all except the most formal occasion (*see* FORMAL DRESS, page 109) a man is safe in a suit. A 'classic' suit is the picture of conservative understatement. It is made in a good quality, dark coloured cloth which is either plain, or patterned with the discreetest stripe or check. The garment is well cut, the jacket hangs well, sleeves end half an inch above shirt cuffs and trousers rest on the shoe. Shirts are white, a pale colour or subtly striped; ties patterned or plain, but generally restrained. Shoes are plain black (no gilt trims); socks dark and unpatterned. Dressed thus, according to the rules, a man will always feel impeccably dressed. Once again, however, it's very much a matter of uniform and everything depends on the life you lead. In different circles such an outfit would be considered decidedly dull or totally inappropriate.

If circumstances are appropriate and nerve permits, there's really nothing to stop a man decking himself out in a snazzy check suit, a gaudy tie or eye-catching shirt or turning up to work in jeans and a jumper.

For many occasions a jacket and trousers are just as acceptable as a suit. Many classier restaurants do still insist on jacket and tie. Check first if in doubt.

Accessories A woman can always wear a hat on dressy occasions and can of course sport one more often if it fits in with her own style. A man should remove his hat when indoors, while a woman keeps hers on if she wants to (except in the theatre or cinema), or take it off if it is likely to get in the way. If you meet someone outdoors and are wearing gloves, take them off before shaking hands if you get a chance (but *see* GLOVES, page 109).

Jewellery for men is a moot point. The base line is a signet ring and plain wrist watch, but the individual can add whatever he thinks he can get away with. Women can ignore old rules about 'no diamonds before six' and add flash and glitter as and when they feel like it, although piles of sparklers are perhaps inappropriate at work.

Dressing for the country Take casual, warm clothes for a country visit: jeans or cords, shirts and jumpers. You'll also need stout walking shoes, possibly wellingtons and a water-proof coat, evening wear and clothes for sports such as tennis if you think you'll need them (*see also* SPORTING EVENTS, page 111). Check with hosts before you pack if in doubt (*see* STAYING OVERNIGHT, page 65).

Q *I held a drinks party recently, and when a friend asked me if we were dressing up, I said 'No, no it's casual'. She turned up in a ratty old tracksuit and trainers, and looked surprised to see me in crêpe trousers and a silk shirt. Where did I go wrong?*

A Fashion vocabularies are so imprecise these days that

one woman's casual wear equates with another's finery. To avoid misunderstandings next time, be specific. Statements such as 'Don't get very dressed up – I'm wearing trousers and a silk shirt', or 'wrap up warmly because we'll be outside for the barbecue. I'm going to wear my tracksuit with a big jumper on top', leave no room for doubt.

Formal dress

An invitation which states 'black tie' means that formal dress is to be worn. 'White tie' is very unusual these days, because so few people own the appropriate clothes.

Black tie Men wear a black dinner jacket, black trousers with braid up the outside of the leg; a white evening shirt with a piqué or pleated front, a black bow tie, black patent shoes and socks. A black cummerbund, or more unusually a black waistcoat, complete the picture. Wear one or the other, never both together.
Women can wear a long or short dress or evening trousers. There are very few occasions when long dresses are *de rigueur*, and if you are in any doubt you should try to find out beforehand.

White tie Men wear a black tailcoat; black trousers which sport two rows of braid up the outside leg; white stiff-fronted piqué shirt with wing collar; white bow tie; black patent or leather shoes.
Women dress as for black tie occasions (*see above*).

Exposure A woman can wear a revealing evening dress to any formal occasion and feel sure that she'll be in the company of a good many others who are also revealing shoulders, bosoms or thighs for all they are worth. Exercise caution however if your hosts are Muslims, and dress with decorum to avoid causing offence.

Gloves Long evening gloves for women are very seldom

essential but, fashion has reintroduced them for balls and dances. The most useful type can be opened at the wrist and rolled back for eating. Keep them on for introductions and dancing and wear rings beneath them, bracelets on top.

Q *We've been invited to a New Year dinner dance and my husband is hiring a dress suit for the occasion. Can he wear an ordinary top coat over it for the journey?*

A The traditional garb consists of a black overcoat, but a dark coat would also do. He should be able to hire a long white silk scarf to give the finishing touch to his outfit.

Special occasions

Weddings At a big traditional white wedding, male guests usually wear morning dress. Phone the bride or her parents and ask if in doubt. Morning dress consists of a black or, more usually, grey tail coat, striped or grey trousers, grey waistcoat, white shirt with wing collar and grey cravat or tie and grey or black top hat. Morning dress may be confined to the men in the bridal party in which case other male guests can wear a lounge suit. Lounge suits are the correct choice for registry office weddings too.

Women wedding guests can wear a dressy frock or suit, and should wear a hat if the men are wearing tails. The same type of outfit can be worn for church or registry office weddings.

Christenings Another chance to dress up. Men should wear a lounge suit, women a smart dress or suit and a hat if they wish. The baby is usually decked from head to toe in white frills and furbelows, in a family christening robe if there is one.

Funerals There's no need any more to wear black, although many people choose dark colours. Even close family members may decide to wear less sombre clothing and this is entirely up to them. Generally men should wear a lounge suit with dark tie and women smart outfits which are not too frivolous.

Memorial services are formal occasions when again men wear suits, women smart clothes in a darkish colour with a hat if they wish.

Q *I've been invited to the wedding of a friend's daughter, even though I haven't seen her for years. I never wear hats as a rule, and am reluctant to buy one specially. What is the etiquette?*

A If the wedding is very formal and the men are wearing tails, you will find that all the women will be wearing hats. But for a less formal wedding, it's purely a matter of preference whether you wear a hat or not. You certainly won't feel or look out of place if you decide to go without one.

Sporting events

Aim for warmth and practicality above everything else. Remember that hats, brollies and sunshades can block the view of others at spectator sports, so be considerate.

Ascot Men should wear a lounge suit, women dress up as much as they like and generally wear a hat. In the Royal Enclosure men generally wear morning dress, women must wear a hat. No cameras are allowed at Royal Ascot.

Cowes At some yacht clubs dress is formal: collar and tie for men, dresses and often hats for women. At evening parties on boats men wear collar and tie, women wear dresses, skirts or trousers and flat shoes which take into account the difficulties of getting aboard. In the daytime, wear rubber soled shoes on board so as not to mark the deck.

Henley Regatta A dressy occasion. Men wear jackets or blazer, a tie or cravat and may not remove their jackets in the

Stewards' Enclosure, no matter how hot the day. Women mostly wear dresses of knee length or longer and hats – no trousers.

Wimbledon   The Royal Box and Members Enclosure call for smart dress, including jackets and ties for men. Elsewhere, dress for comfort and the weather.

Shooting   Warm and waterproof clothes in dark colours (bright ones scare the birds). Strong shoes or wellingtons.

Hunting   If you are invited by a hunt member to join the hunt for a day, ask what you should wear. It is important to get this right so as not to cause offence, but the rules are complicated and vary from hunt to hunt, so do make enquiries first. At a hunt ball tails are usually worn, otherwise dinner jackets.

Q   *I have been invited to go sailing for a weekend. What clothes do I need?*

A   First priority is shoes with a non-slip rubber sole. Proper oilskin waterproofs are another must and you may be able to borrow these. Jeans and warm sweaters go underneath. Take a swimsuit, and pack a complete change of clothing just in case of accidents. Pack the lot in a roll-up waterproof bag which can be stashed away on board.

Entertainments

Gone are the days when a night at the opera or theatre was a glittering occasion, the audience in full evening dress. Now it's perfectly acceptable to dress casually for either, although those in more expensive seats tend to dress up a bit more. First nights and galas are different and call for a dressier outfit.

Glyndebourne   Sussex opera festival, held every summer.

Black tie and long evening dress are usual, although lounge suit and short dresses are permitted. Take a cover-up of some sort for outdoor strolling or picnicking and an umbrella.

Covent Garden   Dress up if you like. Fairly casual dress is acceptable.

Q *My father is treating me with tickets for the opera at the London Coliseum. We are sitting in the stalls. Do I need to wear an evening dress?*

A The London Coliseum is less formal than Covent Garden, so a very glamorous evening dress would not be appropriate. However, most people in the stalls will have dressed up a little for the occasion, so choose less formal evening gear and you won't go wrong.

8

Etiquette for every occasion

None of us can altogether escape the rituals that surround life's landmarks: birth, marriage and death. The ceremonies that accompany these events are full of ancient significance and even if you pooh-pooh them as a lot of fuss and bother, it's not hard to see why people cling to the continuity of tradition, and want to recognize important occasions with due ceremony. Most people would probably agree that it would be a shame if all the old rites were to disappear. That said, if you are organizing or attending a christening, wedding or funeral you will need to know what to do and what to expect. The same goes even more so for guests at ceremonies and celebrations belonging to cultures with which they are unfamiliar.

Births and christenings

Announcing a birth   Broadcast the news of a baby's birth in the time-honoured fashion with an excited phone call to close relatives, plus phone calls or notes to friends. As a follow-up you can advertise the arrival in the newspaper. Copy the style of other announcements in the paper of your choice, or use one of the examples given here:

King On 15 November at Bridgnorth Hospital, to Susan and Peter, a son, Robert James.

King On 15 November at Bridgnorth Hospital, to Susan (nee Farnsworth) and Peter, a son.

Farnsworth and King On 15 November at Bridgnorth Hospital, to Susan Farnsworth and Peter King, a son.

Planning a christening A christening is the ceremony which welcomes a baby into the Christian faith, on the understanding that the child will be given a Christian upbringing, and in the hope that he or she will affirm that faith when older. It can take place as part of another Sunday ceremony, or may be held separately. Talk to your vicar or priest about his preferred arrangements, as these will vary from church to church.

Christenings are usually fairly small gatherings, involving family and close friends only. The child's parents should think carefully about the choice of godparents. Traditionally a child has one of each sex in the Roman Catholic church, while in the Church of England the quota is two godfathers and one godmother for a boy, vice versa for a girl. Some parents choose to nominate more than the minimum number of godparents.

A good godparent will take a special interest in the child's welfare as he or she grows up, and the task should not be accepted lightly. During the ceremony the godparents are asked to confirm their own faith, and the church may require that they be practising Christians who have been baptized and confirmed.

Parents should ask the chosen godparents if they are prepared to stand, some time in advance of the ceremony. Anyone who is asked to be a godparent but is for any reason unprepared to take on the role, should say so tactfully at once, rather than accepting reluctantly without being prepared to fulfil the obligation properly over the years to come.

Private christenings, which do not form part of another service, usually take place in the afternoon, in which case it is customary to follow them with a tea. A christening cake is usually served, which may even be the re-iced top tier of the wedding cake, and a toast may be drunk in champagne. All those who attended the service, including the priest or vicar, should be invited. A small lunch or drinks party would be just as appropriate if the christening forms part of a morning or early evening service.

Christening gifts   Presents are given by close family and godparents, although other guests might like to bring a small gift. Gifts need not be large or lavish, but should be lasting reminders of the occasion for the future: a silver or bone china gift; jewellery for a girl; good wine or port that will come to maturity when the child is old enough to enjoy it; a shrub or tree. You can also give money in the form of a cheque or Premium Bonds, or perhaps invested in an account opened specially in the child's name.

The baby's parents should send a thank-you note within a few days of the ceremony to everyone who brings a gift. And guests should thank the parents for their hospitality with a note or phone call.

Q *I would like to ask my uncle to be godfather at my baby's christening in February, but he suffers from bouts of bronchitis during the winter which keep him indoors, and I am afraid he might not be able to attend the ceremony. Is there any way round the problem?*

A Your uncle can nominate a friend or other relative to stand proxy for him if he is not well enough to be there. If this happens, you should mention it to the clergyman before the ceremony begins so there is no confusion.

Engagements

Making the announcement   The question has been asked, the answer is yes – what happens next? The old tradition, by which the man had to ask the woman's father for her hand in marriage, has virtually died out, but it is courteous for the couple to make sure that the woman's parents are the first to be told the news. They should do this in person if at all possible, rather than over the phone. Second on the list should be the man's family, and it is a wise idea to arrange for the two families to meet as soon as possible, if they have not done so already. Traditionally, the bride's mother writes to the parents of the groom, suggesting a meeting.

If either partner is widowed, he or she should write to the late spouse's family to tell them of the engagement. In the case of a previous divorce, it is courteous but not essential to inform the ex-spouse's family if you are on good terms with them. This becomes more important when there are children of the first marriage who may gain an extra set of grandparents.

Word of an engagement will soon get round to other family and friends. The couple can tell people informally on the phone or with a short note, and can also announce their engagement in a newspaper if they wish. The following are examples of different wordings which can be used, depending on circumstances.

Mr K J Owen and Miss S L Davidson

The engagement is announced between Kevin, younger son of Mr and Mrs Arthur Owen of Lincoln, and Sally, second daughter of Mr and Mrs Ivan Davidson of Grantham, Lincs.

Mr C J Lear and Miss M R McCabe

The engagement is announced, and the marriage will take place on 25 November in London, between Christopher James, elder son of the late Mr F W Lear and Mrs P T Smythe of Worcester and Marianne Ruth, only daughter of Mr and Mrs Leonard McCabe of Arundel, Sussex. *(The groom's father is dead, and his mother has remarried.)*

Mr A J Fox and Miss E L Marvin *(or Mrs E L Barlow if the woman is a widow, or has retained her married name after divorce)*

The engagement is announced between Anthony Fox and Eileen Marvin, both of Bristol. *(Suitable wording for a second marriage. The couple could mention their parents' names as well, if they wished.)*

Engagement parties The couple might like to organize a small dinner where both sets of parents can get to know each other, or may prefer to have a larger party for all their friends. A toast would be drunk at a party, but there is no necessity for speeches, which can be saved for the wedding. Thank guests for engagement presents as they are given, and send a thank-you note as well.

Broken engagements There is no obligation to explain why an engagement has been broken. Relatives and friends may be told by letter or phone and any engagement presents which have been received should be returned to the giver, with a short note of thanks. The woman should give back her ring to the man, and both should return any gifts received from each other. (*See also* CANCELLING A WEDDING, page 121.)

Q *Is your wedding ring worn inside or outside your engagement ring? A friend told me recently that the engagement ring goes on first, so that you never have to remove it, but I always thought it was the other way round.*

A Traditionally you should wear your wedding ring inside your engagement ring (ie your wedding ring goes on first). During the marriage ceremony the engagement ring is worn on the right hand, leaving the left hand's ring finger free to receive the wedding ring.

Q *My fiancé has given me a beautiful antique ring, set with a row of six stones, in different colours. Can you tell me what the origin of the design might be?*

A Your ring is probably a 'REGARD' ring, which was popular with the Victorians. The initials of each stone: ruby, emerald, garnet, amethyst, ruby, diamond, spelt out the word. Sometimes rings were specially made so that the stones spelt out the name of the woman's fiancé. Traditionally, the different precious stones had meanings: diamonds stood for lasting love; emeralds for happiness; sapphires for wisdom and rubies for contentment.

Weddings

In order to marry, both partners must be aged over sixteen, and those under eighteen will need the consent of parents or guardian. Divorced people may not remarry until the decree absolute has come through.

The first step is to set the date, which will probably need to be at least six months hence, as most churches and popular reception venues get booked up well in advance.

Next decision is how lavish a ceremony and reception to have. Money plays a big part here of course. In the past the bride's family bore the burden of cost, but these days many couples finance their own wedding, and both families chip in.

Invitations These are usually specially printed, and any reputable stationer will be able to show you samples. Standard wording is shown on page 47 (*see also* APPENDIX, page 136).

If the bride's parents are divorced, they may still decide to present a united front for the wedding day, in which case the invitations are worded: Mr Alastair Jamieson and Mrs Sheila Jamieson (or Mrs Samuel McKintyre, if the bride's mother has remarried) request the pleasure of your company at the marriage of their daughter...'

Should one of the bride's parents be dead, invitations come from the surviving parent: 'Mrs Derek Tucker requests...' In the case of a remarriage of the bride's widowed parent, invitations come from: 'Mr and Mrs Alan Rusbridge request the pleasure of your company at the marriage of his/her daughter...' In these circumstances it may ease any confusion if the bride's surname is included on invitations.

Those who are marrying for the second time may well want to send invitations in their own names: Mr Tim Buchanan and Miss Rosa Hartley request the pleasure of your company at their marriage.... Second timers are not allowed to marry in church if one or both of them is divorced while their former spouse/s are still living, but a sympathetic clergyman may permit them to have a ceremony of blessing after a civil marriage. In this case, the invitations can be to '... a Ceremony of Blessing following their marriage...'

With registry office weddings, where space is limited, it may be possible to invite only a few people to the ceremony, and ask more to come to the reception. In this case the wording can read: '...the pleasure of your company to the reception following the marriage...'

Who to invite Space and budget will determine the maximum number of guests and bride and groom have a good opportunity to practise the essential art of compromise when drawing up the guest list. One possibility if the numbers are in danger of getting out of hand is to have a small wedding and reception for family and close friends only, and hold a larger party for other friends and colleagues later on.

Are you happy for friends with young children or babies to bring them along? If not, it's tactful to have a word with them and explain your feelings, rather than risk a misunderstanding. Guests who receive a wedding invitation which does not mention their children, should assume that the children are not invited.

If one partner has been divorced, it is more considerate to the new partner not to invite members of the ex's family (and almost certainly not the ex in person, no matter how amicable you are). Apart from any other considerations, if there are too many significant faces from the past, your guests will start to suffer from *déjà vu*.

Another potentially tricky area arises when the parents of bride or groom are divorced and one or both of them has remarried. Members of the step-family should be invited, although the guest list will depend to a certain extent on the feelings among the family. The happiest solution is to bury any hatchets for the day, invite everyone and rely on them all to behave in a civilized manner. (*See* WHO SITS WHERE, page 123).

Wedding presents   Many couples put together a 'wedding list' itemizing gifts they would like to receive, which is placed with a particular store, or sent to guests who ask for a copy. However, there is no need for guests to feel bound by the list if they have a more idiosyncratic gift in mind.

Everyone who attends the wedding should give a present, which need not be large, but should of course be thoughtfully chosen. Guests should preferably send the gift to the address on the wedding invitation beforehand, or take it along on the day, making sure it is clearly and securely marked with the donor's name. The recipients should keep a careful check on who gives what, so that the right people are thanked for the right present.

Donors should receive a written thank you (see page 42 for an example) as soon as possible after sending the gift, and bride/groom should write to those who bring gifts on the day immediately after their return from honeymoon.

Cancelling or postponing a wedding   As with a broken engagement, there is no need to offer explanations for calling off a wedding. An advertisement can be placed in the press, saying simply 'The marriage arranged between Mr Simon Webster and Miss Madeleine Walker will not now take place', but this is not essential. The parents of the bride should tell close family and friends by phone or letter.

If the wedding is called off when invitations have already gone out, printed cancellation cards or informal notes can be sent out to all guests. Don't leave this to chance if the cancellation happens at the eleventh hour. Better to telephone guests if there isn't time to contact them by post.

Any wedding gifts that have been received should be returned to the giver, with a brief note of thanks.

Very occasionally a wedding has to be postponed, usually due to the serious illness or death of a close relative. Cards should be sent to the guests, telling them the reason for the postponement and notifying them of the new date if this is known and is not too far hence. 'It is deeply regretted that due to the death of Mr Daniel O'Connor the marriage of his daughter Mary to Mr Tim Cunningham on 16 July 1988 has been postponed.'

Etiquette for second marriages Widows and widowers may remarry in church, but divorced people may not, although they may be permitted to have a blessing in church following a registry office wedding. In either case, a white dress and the trappings of a first marriage are inappropriate, and the bride should dress in an attractive outfit of her own choice, the groom in a lounge suit. The reception can follow similar lines to that for a first marriage, with cake, toasts and speeches (*see below*).

The wedding ceremony

For a wedding in church the bride and groom will have to choose attendants, each of whom has a role to play.

The best man Traditionally the best man organizes the stag night, which should preferably not be held on the night before the wedding, since it is also up to the best man to ensure that the groom is in a fit state for the ceremony. He also has to organize the groom on the day, making sure he arrives at the church in good time. The best man takes charge of the wedding ring, handing it over at the appropriate moment in the ceremony, and may also be needed to check that buttonholes, orders of service and so on are ready at the church to be given to guests. He pays any church fees due on the day on behalf of the groom, ensures that the groom's honeymoon luggage is taken to the reception venue, takes charge of the groom's wedding clothes after the reception, returning them if hired. He also makes a speech at the reception (*see* SPEECHES AND TOASTS, page 125) and generally helps to make sure things run smoothly.

The ushers They stand at the door of the church and direct guests to their seats (*see* WHO SITS WHERE, page 123), handing out orders of service or hymn books and buttonholes. One usher should personally show the bride's mother to her place. Ushers can escort the bridesmaids from the church after the ceremony, and should help the best man to make sure that all the guests have transport to the reception.

The bridesmaids and pageboys　The chief bridesmaid gives the bride support and help. It is her job to keep any young attendants in order and make sure they behave during the ceremony. She may help the bride to dress and check that her honeymoon luggage is sent to the reception. She goes to the church before the bride and arranges the bride's dress and veil at the door. During the marriage she holds the bride's bouquet, and may help her to lift her veil back. At the end of the reception she helps the bride get changed, and takes charge of her wedding dress.

Who sits where　As guests arrive at church the ushers should ask them if they should sit on the bride's or groom's side of the church. The bride's family and friends occupy the left-hand side of the church and the groom's sit on the right. The front right pew is occupied by the groom's parents, with best man and groom beside the aisle, ready to stand when the bride enters. The bride's mother sits in the front left pew, and the bride's father joins her there after he has given the bride away. Other relatives sit behind, and friends sit at the back.

If the divorced parents of bride or groom join forces for the day, they should sit together. Second husbands or wives and children of second marriages, if invited, should play a low-key role in the day and sit with the friends or relatives of bride or groom.

The Ceremony　It makes very good sense to have a rehearsal of the ceremony a day or two before the wedding itself for the couple, bride's father and attendants, so that everyone knows exactly what to do, when to stand, sit and kneel and so on.

On the day, the bride is last to arrive at the church with her father, and enters the church on his right arm. If her father is no longer alive she can be given away by another close male relative. If the bride is a widow she may choose not to be given away, but should still be escorted down the aisle.

At the appropriate moment in the ceremony the groom places the ring on the bride's finger. The couple may choose to exchange rings at this point.

After the marriage the register has to be signed and the couple, their parents and the attendants including the best man should proceed to the vestry to do this.

Registry office weddings

The couple will be asked to sign a declaration that there is no legal reason why they should not marry. Both partners must have lived locally to the registry office for seven days, unless they are married by licence.

Two witnesses only are needed, but most couples like to invite a small party of guests who should be asked to arrive around fifteen minutes before the ceremony. The couple should arrive five to ten minutes before the scheduled time. The registrar will call the couple in on their own first, explain the proceedings to them and collect the fee. The guests then join the couple for the ceremony, which lasts around ten minutes and ends with the signing of the register.

It is unusual for a large, formal reception to be held following a registry office wedding and many couples prefer to have an informal lunch or evening party.

The reception

Guests are generally greeted at a reception by a receiving line which includes bride and groom and their parents plus attendants and best man. If a sit-down meal is being served the top table is occupied by bride and groom, their parents and the best man and chief bridesmaid. For a very large gathering it's best to have a seating plan prominently on show. It is no longer usual to display gifts, but they can be set out if there is space.

Speeches and toasts After the meal the bride's father rises and makes a speech which should sum up his pleasure on this happy occasion and end with a toast proposed to the bride and groom. The groom responds with thanks on behalf of his wife and himself to everyone who has been involved in the organization of the wedding and ends by proposing a toast to the bridesmaids. Finally the best man has his chance to shine with a witty speech, following which he reads out any messages and cards which have been received. Next he announces that the cake will be cut. The bride and groom make the first cut with due ceremony and the cake is then removed and cut into small pieces which are handed round to guests. Pieces can be packed up and sent to absent friends later on.

All that remains at the end of the reception is for the bride and groom to change. The best man announces their departure, the bride throws her bouquet into the throng, and the couple drive, or are driven away in a shower of confetti.

After the wedding A wedding is one of the few occasions where it is not necessary for guests to write and formally thank their hosts, although naturally they will express their appreciation as they leave the reception.

A press notice can be inserted after the wedding, using wording in the style of the chosen newspaper, which will be along the following lines:

Mr A M Young and Miss J Troughton

The marriage took place on 15 April at Brighton, Sussex, of Mr Andrew Young, son of Mr and Mrs W Young, and Miss Josephine Troughton, younger daughter of Mr and Mrs F Troughton of Eastbourne, Sussex.

Q *We've decided to push the boat out and have a big wedding, with over 200 guests. Is it all right to keep them waiting to greet the receiving line at the start of the reception, or can we visit each table later on to make sure we have spoken to everyone?*

A It's better to accept the fact that people will have to wait for a few minutes when they arrive at the reception, because later on it's unlikely that everyone would get a chance to speak to you and your parents. You could make the queuing easier by serving champagne or sherry to guests as they wait.

Q *A colleague has invited each of us in the office to her wedding. There is a move afoot to contribute a small amount each to buy her a joint present, but I think we should give her separate, individual gifts.*

A Since you've each received a personal invitation, you should each give an individual gift. If a joint gift is given, why don't you contribute a small amount, and give an additional present yourself.

Q *A friend sent me a charming thank-you letter after her wedding – but for the wrong gift. Should I keep quiet, or tell her of the mistake?*

A Do mention it, because in all probability someone else has been thanked for *your* gift, so the misunderstanding needs to be cleared up. Be pleasant about it and just ring or write, saying 'Thank you for your lovely letter – but I did think you should know...'

Funerals

When someone dies, close relatives, friends and colleagues should be told straight away, by telephone or letter. They should respond by writing immediately to whoever has been bereaved (*see* LETTERS OF CONDOLENCE, page 42 for an example, and also for how to acknowledge letters of sympathy). Depending on how soon the funeral is to take place, letters can indicate whether or not the writer will be able to attend. There should be no hesitation in offering help with arrangements or catering if practicable.

A notice can be placed in the press, and the newspaper of your choice will be able to help with wording, which can be along the following lines:

McArthur – on August 5, at Haysfield Hospital, Malcolm George, aged 78 years. Funeral at St Mary's church, Haysfield on August 14 at 2.30pm.

Flowers   If flowers are not acceptable at the funeral, any press announcement will make this clear. Otherwise, flowers can be sent to the undertakers, or on the day of the funeral to the house from which the funeral is taking place. A card should be attached, saying who sent the flowers and bearing a suitable message such as 'With fondest love'.

You may know that the deceased person belonged to a particular religion with which you are unfamiliar. Most religions have customs surrounding funerals – for instance, sending Mass cards for a Roman Catholic – and if you are in any doubt as to what is appropriate, it's a good idea to ring a local representative of that religion at the place of worship and ask what you should do.

Sometimes the deceased person has made it known during his or her life that donations to a particular charity would be preferable to flowers and this information should be given in any press announcements.

The funeral   Invitations as such are not issued for funerals. Friends or relatives whom the family of the deceased think might like to come can be contacted direct and given details. See page 110, for details of what to wear to a funeral.

Family mourners generally meet at the house of the deceased, and the coffin, if not there already, will be brought in a hearse from the undertakers, to lead the cars to the funeral. Others attending the service gather at the church or chapel.

During the service the closest relatives usually sit in the front pews, with friends and relatives behind. At a burial it is customary for the family mourners only to go to the graveside, but sometimes the entire congregation will attend this part of the ceremony.

After the funeral it is usual to offer refreshment such as tea or a light lunch to some or all of those attending, particularly if they have travelled a long distance. This usually takes place at the home of the bereaved.

Memorial services   Some families like to keep the funeral small and intimate and follow it several weeks later with a service in remembrance of the dead person, attended by a larger number of people. Notice of a memorial service can be published in the press:

Jonas: A service of thanksgiving for the life and work of Dr Erica Jonas will be held in Norwich Cathedral, on Tuesday 6 December at 11am.

What to say to someone who has been bereaved   Many people feel embarrassed or unsure of what to say when they first meet someone after a bereavement, and may say nothing simply because they don't know what words to use. It is however far better to acknowledge the other person's loss than to pretend nothing has happened, which can seem very hurtful and insensitive. Saying 'I was so sorry to hear about your mother...', leaves it up to the other person either to say simply 'Thank you', or to talk more about their bereavement if they wish.

Q *Although we specified that donations be made to the hospital where my father was so well-treated during his last illness, I learned later that several of his colleagues had collected some money and given it to various charities selected between them. Shouldn't they have respected our wishes in this?*

A No doubt they meant well, but yes, unless a press

notice says 'contributions to charities of your choice', people should make donations to the organization specified by the family.

Ceremonies of other cultures

Being invited to a ceremony celebrated by people of a different nationality or religion is a privilege and a fascinating opportunity to gain insight into a different culture. Whatever your own beliefs and customs, you are likely to find that there are significant differences in the way a ceremony is conducted from what you are used to. It is as well to find out what to expect in advance.

The simplest way to do this is to ask the friend or colleague who has invited you what form the ceremony will take, if there are any special customs or taboos you should be aware of, particularly involving what to wear (you may be expected to cover your head, for instance, or remove your shoes), what you can eat or drink, and any rules involving male and female segregation (in an Orthodox synagogue, for example). Most people will be only too happy to explain the rituals belonging to their own particular culture, and may be able to arrange for you to be seated near someone who can guide you on what to do if necessary.

If for any reason you can't ask your hosts, you would still be well advised to do some preliminary research. You could ring the appropriate local church or other centre of worship, or telephone the embassy of the appropriate country to ask for more information.

Q *Jewish friends have asked us to attend their son's bar mitzvah. What is the purpose of this ceremony?*

A It is to celebrate the fact that the boy has reached the age of thirteen, when he is considered an adult and can take part in prayers and synagogue service. He will have studied long and hard for the great day, and after the service you should shake his hand and congratulate him. The bar mitzvah will probably take place during the Saturday morning service, and may be mainly in Hebrew or English, depending on whether your friends are Orthodox Jews or belong to the Reform or Liberal groups. Afterwards there will be a dinner of kosher food for all the guests, at which the boy will make a speech. You should take a present for him. If in doubt as to what to give, ask his parents for suggestions.

9

Very special occasions

Every once in a while an invitation arrives to an ultra-formal or official occasion which is quite outside a person's normal run-of-the-mill sphere of activity. Whether the event is a banquet, ceremony or garden party it will almost certainly follow a prescribed pattern.

Formal functions

A banquet hosted by the local mayor (or even the Lord Mayor); a trade function; a military dinner – all of these have their own peculiarities about dress and custom which are far too varied and complicated to give in detail here. At many such occasions traditional custom, ceremony and protocol will be observed and if you are unfamiliar with what to expect the best bet is to ring the office of the person or organization who issued the invitation and ask for more details. On the day itself watch what others do and follow suit.

The invitation to a formal function will invariably be couched in formal language and you should reply in similar style (*see* REPLYING TO FORMAL INVITATIONS, page 48).

The invitation may give a clue as to what to wear (*see* page 109, BLACK TIE and WHITE TIE). If you are in any doubt, ring the organizers beforehand and ask.

You may know in advance that you will be introduced to a titled person and if that is likely it pays to do your homework and find out the correct way in which to address him or her. Your library should have a copy of *Debrett's Correct Form*, which can supply all the detail you will need.

Basically, behave as you would at any function. Make an effort to remember people's names, and talk to the guests on either side of you at the dinner table, giving preference to neither. Grace may be said before the meal, so don't start eating until you see others doing so. At a formal banquet with many courses, use the cutlery starting from the outside and working inwards (*see* CUTLERY, page 90 for more details). Glasses will be filled for you as appropriate and you can refuse drink or a course of food if you wish.

At the end of a dinner port may be served and the decanter should be passed round the table to the left. Watch to see if your fellow guests start drinking before you take a sip, since they may be waiting for the loyal toast which is drunk to 'The Queen'. Toasts themselves vary greatly. They come at the end of the meal and may be brief or preceded by a lengthy speech. Some toasts are drunk while seated, for others you stand. You should refrain from smoking until after the toasts.

Try not to be too nervous if you are invited to a very formal occasion. There is a lot of fun to be had out of participating and observing the strange old customs and rituals, so go prepared to enjoy yourself.

Q *I have been invited to a Lord Mayor's banquet next month. Unfortunately, I have to travel north the same night for an important meeting which starts early the next morning, and think that I may have to leave the banquet early in order to catch the last train. Is it in order just to get up and leave while the meal is still in progress?*

A No, unfortunately it is not, and you will have to make a choice. Either refuse the invitation to the banquet, or make alternative arrangements about your meeting, such as staying overnight in a hotel near the station and catching a very early train, or arriving after the meeting has started.

Royal occasions

Since the royal family have such a high public profile, and are so frequently out and about meeting their subjects, it is perfectly feasible for many people to have the opportunity to meet one or other of the royals. This might happen at a formal function or during an informal visit to home town or place of work. As with so much else in life, etiquette surrounding the royal family is far less formal than in the the past, but it is still as well to know what to say and do should you find yourself confronted with a regal presence.

What to do and say   Royal visits and functions are highly organized affairs, and those who are to be presented to royalty will be warned well in advance that this is going to happen. A member of the royal family should be called 'Your Royal Highness' (or 'Your Majesty' for the Queen and Queen Mother) when you first speak to her or him, and thereafter called 'Ma'am' (to rhyme with jam), or 'Sir'. When presented to royalty, men should bow the head and women should curtsey or bow likewise, shaking hands only if the royal hand is proffered.

Old rules about speaking only when spoken to by a monarch, and not asking questions, have generally gone by the board, although you should be polite and not embark on difficult topics of conversation or ask personal questions. In theory, you should call a member of the royal family 'Your Royal Highness' in conversation, rather than 'you' (as in 'Your Royal Highness may remember that . . .'). Certainly in a formal speech given in the presence of royalty you should use this form to refer to the royal guests. But in informal conversation the rule can be relaxed.

Remain on your feet if royalty are standing, don't ask for an autograph, and do not leave the gathering until royalty has left (although this rule is waived at banquets and garden parties).

Accepting and refusing royal invitations   An invitation from royalty should be taken as a command, and should not be refused except for exceptional reasons. The invitation itself will be worded formally and will come from a member of the royal household, not from the Queen herself. Your reply should be handwritten and can read as follows:

Mr and Mrs L R Morrison thank the Master of the Household
[or whoever sent the invitation] for the invitation to the State
Banquet and have the honour to obey Her Majesty's command on 19 April at 7.30pm.

To refuse an invitation, use the following wording:

Mr & Mrs L R Morrison thank the Master of the Household
for the invitation to the State Banquet, but regret that they
will be unable to attend due to the serious illness of Mrs
Morrison.

Inviting royalty To invite a member of the royal family to a
function which you are organizing, such as an official opening, first telephone the Private Secretary at Buckingham
Palace to ascertain whether or not your invitation is likely to
be accepted, and whether your proposed date is possible. If
you are given the go ahead at this stage, write to the Private
Secretary to confirm the invitation.

Garden parties There are four royal garden parties each
year, three at Buckingham Palace and one at Holyrood
House, Edinburgh. Invitations to these arrive complete with
full directions on where to park and where to go, plus an
admission card. There is no need to write and accept a garden
party invitation, but if you have to refuse you should return
the admission card with your letter of regret.

Men can wear morning dress or a uniform, but many wear
lounge suits. Women dress up in smart dresses and most
choose to wear hats. Go prepared with umbrella if the
weather is uncertain and wear shoes which are comfortable
enough for a fair amount of walking.

Many people attend garden parties, and a fairly small
number only are presented to the royal family during the
course of the afternoon.

Royal Ascot To receive vouchers for the Royal Enclosure,
applicants should write formally to The Ascot Office, St
James's Palace, London SW1 between 1 January and 30 April,

saying: 'Mr & Mrs J W Searle present their compliments and beg the honour of vouchers for the Royal Enclosure at Ascot.' You will be sent a form which must be completed and signed by a sponsor who has him or herself been invited several times in the past. None of this is a guarantee of success, as demand for vouchers outstrips supply.

If you are lucky, remember that you will have to comply with strict rules about dress on the day (*see* SPORTING EVENTS: ASCOT, page 111, for details).

Other royal occasions The public may have other opportunities to mingle with royalty at State banquets, investitures and awards ceremonies. The royal household is so experienced in successful organization, that invitations to any of these events will generally also give details of precisely what to wear and where to go at what time.

Q *The Prince of Wales is coming to open my firm's new factory and I have been asked to present members of my department to him. What do I say when I make the introduction?*

A You will have been asked beforehand to provide details of those people whom you wish to present to the Prince. All you need to say is: 'Your Royal Highness, may I present Miss Sarah Adams.' You'll find that the royal staff will organize the whole event to run very smoothly, and will be able to advise on any other problems or questions.

Q *My wife and I are due to attend a garden party this summer. Should we write and thank the Queen afterwards?*

A Strictly speaking this is unnecessary, but there's nothing to stop you doing so, and your letter will be seen by the Queen.

Appendix

Below, are some variations on the standard wording for wedding invitations (see page 46 for further information).

Mr and Mrs Michael Spencer
request the pleasure of your company
at the marriage of their daughter
Helen Julia
to
Mr James Thompson
at St Peter's Church, Cambridge
on Saturday 14th August
at 3 o'clock
and afterwards at
The Royal Hotel, Queen Street,
Cambridge

RSVP
10 London Road
Cambridge

Mr and Mrs Michael Spencer
request the pleasure of the company of

....

at the marriage of their daughter
Helen Julia
to
Mr James Thompson
at
St Peter's Church, Cambridge
on
Saturday 14th August
at 3 o'clock
and afterwards at
The Royal Hotel, Queen Street, Cambridge

RSVP
10 London Road
Cambridge

James and Helen
invite

to their marriage
at
St. Peter's Church, Cambridge
on
Saturday 14th August
at
3 o' clock
and afterwards at
the Royal Hotel, Queen Street, Cambridge

~ RSVP ~
10 London Road
Cambridge

James and Helen
invite

to the reception following their marriage
at
the Royal Hotel, Queen Street, Cambridge
on
Saturday 14th August
at 8 p.m.

R S V P
10 London Road
Cambridge

Index